WELCOME
TO AI

WELCOME TO AI

A Human Guide to
Artificial Intelligence

DAVID L. SHRIER

HARVARD BUSINESS REVIEW PRESS
BOSTON, MASSACHUSETTS

The web addresses referenced in this book were live and correct at the time of the book's publication but may be subject to change.

Library of Congress Cataloging-in-Publication Data

Names: Shrier, David L., author.
Title: Welcome to AI : a human guide to artificial intelligence / David L. Shrier.
Description: Boston, Massachusetts : Harvard Business Review Press, [2024] |
    Includes index.
Identifiers: LCCN 2023046177 (print) | LCCN 2023046178 (ebook) |
    ISBN 9781647827526 (hardcover) | ISBN 9781647827533 (epub)
Subjects: LCSH: Vocational guidance. | Artificial intelligence—Social aspects. |
    Artificial intelligence—Vocational guidance. | Artificial intelligence—
    Industrial applications—Vocational guidance.
Classification: LCC HF5381 .S5783 2024 (print) | LCC HF5381 (ebook) |
    DDC 650.14—dc23/eng/20231003
LC record available at https://lccn.loc.gov/2023046177
LC ebook record available at https://lccn.loc.gov/2023046178

ISBN: 978-1-64782-752-6
eISBN: 978-1-64782-753-3

The paper used in this publication meets the requirements of the American National Standard for Permanence of Paper for Publications and Documents in Libraries and Archives Z39.48-1992.

To those who believe in a better tomorrow

Imagination is the only weapon
in the war with reality.

—Lewis Carroll, *Alice's Adventures in Wonderland*

CONTENTS

Introduction

We live in interesting times.

Bear in mind that the period of the Black Death was an interesting time, as was the Hundred Years War. Of course, the Italian Renaissance was also an interesting time, and so was the Golden Age of China.

What is clear is that we are in a period of historic change, as human society faces a transformative force unlike any other it has previously faced, a new technology that perhaps may more profoundly affect the course of human history than the invention of the wheel, agriculture, or the steam engine.

I speak, of course, of artificial intelligence (AI).

Already, AI has changed the course of global politics and, for better or worse, threatened US hegemony. It has introduced new uncertainty into financial markets. It has suddenly become a topic of conversation in boardrooms around the world. AI has the potential to reshape the geopolitical landscape. Now, a smaller nation like Switzerland, the United Kingdom, Singapore, or Israel can be on level footing with superpowers like the United States and China. It's the new nuclear age, but instead of splitting atoms, we're chasing electrons.

Every week brings with it a new story of a major corporation or even nation making or anticipating significant changes brought about by AI. While I was writing this book, the CEO of BT Group (formerly British Telecom) announced that he intended to replace 40 percent of his workforce with AI, reducing it by up to 55,000 people by 2030.[1]

Discussing the final draft with a colleague, he revealed he was about to raise $1 billion (all references to dollars are to US currency) for a new venture capital fund focused on AI, and he had already negotiated his first sixty investments.

As I finished a few final summary elements, news came out that a lawyer with thirty years of experience was facing potential sanctions for having submitted a brief created by the generative AI system ChatGPT that included fake citations about cases that never existed.

In the middle of a sweltering summer day, shortly after I submitted copyedits, over 150 colleagues joined me in a classroom on the Imperial College campus in South Kensington, as well as over Zoom, to discuss how we adapt our teaching to address the changes imposed by AI.

I wrote my first AI software program in 1991. It wasn't terribly exciting; I was using software in order to simulate what a particular type of neural network computer would do if it, in fact, existed. Even twenty years later, in 2011, AI was interesting technology, but fairly arcane and challenging to navigate.

Three events occurred within the past few years that changed everything.

The first was largely unnoticed outside of technology circles: in 2015, Google published a powerful library of AI technology known as TensorFlow into the open source.[2] Now, large numbers of programmers had access to sophisticated AI models and capabilities that previously were restricted to big tech, big academia, some governments, and a handful of well-funded startups. This gave rise to a generation of startups whose technology is now coming out from development.

The second event was likewise unheralded outside of computer science circles, when Google returned to the discussion with the publication of BERT into open source in late 2018.[3] BERT stands for Bidirectional Encoder Representations from Transformers. Transformers are a fundamental AI technology that make the current AI revolution possible.

The third event, which was a direct consequence of the first two, has been making regular headlines since December 2022. OpenAI, a company that Elon Musk helped form with Y Combinator impresario Sam Altman and a few others, released a public-facing interface to its large language model (LLM) artificial intelligence. Known as ChatGPT, this system served as an electric jolt to the nervous system of business and society at large. Rapidly adopted by people numbering in the hundreds of millions, it revealed the potential of AI in a way people had not previously been capable of understanding. It brought the power of advanced AI to people in a fashion that was as easy to use as a search engine.

Our world is changing rapidly as a result of this AI revolution. Speaking for my own advisory practice at Visionary Future, the inquiries began coming weekly, now daily, from all corners. Everyone from a top-ten investment bank to one of the three fastest-growing tech companies in Europe has reached out to seek guidance on how to apply AI, what the new and emerging developments mean in the context of their businesses and those of their clients, and what new competitive threats might come about as a result of this disruption.

The private sector is only part of my life. I've also dedicated a significant portion of my life to public service in my efforts to apply technologies to solve problems at scale.

In my work in academia, my colleagues at Imperial College London and I, as well as those at the University of Oxford, the Massachusetts Institute of Technology (MIT), the University of Edinburgh, and elsewhere, share a common concern that in the race to adopt AI, we need to ensure the direction we take is good for humanity. We are working to bring about AI systems we can rely on, that will improve the lot of everyone. We want to create the Trusted AI Alliance to promote this idea, an initiative spanning more than 3,000 researchers (to start with) who are ready to tackle this problem. It's imperative to the future of the human race because if we get it wrong, we could create catastrophic consequences for society. Worse than the Black Death, worse than the Second World War, more far-reaching than the Industrial Revolution.

With this in mind, I seek to provide you with a handy field guide to the world of AI so you can inform your own decisions about what to do, how to go about it, and what the risks are of inaction.

This book is brief, of necessity, although I have provided some guideposts if you wish to explore more deeply.

Let's start with the basics . . .

PART I

AI CHANGES EVERYTHING

Part I focuses on the fundamentals: What is AI? How has it impacted us thus far? What risks does it present in the workplace?

1

Rise of the Bots and AI Hallucinations

- ChatGPT has upended the artificial intelligence playing field, acquiring hundreds of millions of users in a matter of months.

- AI systems already have had significant geopolitical impacts, such as on Brexit and the 2016 US presidential election.

- Caution is warranted with AI because it can be prone to *hallucinations* of a sort.

"What are you going to do about ChatGPT?"

The then-dean of Imperial College Business School, Francisco Veloso, asked me the question almost casually when I stopped by his office. It was January 2023. The storm clouds of artificial intelligence were breaking open over the staid world of academia. Because my professorial title says "AI & Innovation" and my signature class that I created for Imperial College London teaches students how to launch new AI startups, I was expected to have an answer.

Others in university circles were up in arms. Ban the technology! Use plagiarism software to detect if students were cheating with ChatGPT! Reactions from professors worldwide were strong.

ChatGPT is a consumer-facing service that allows you to engage in conversation with an AI and have it not only give you answers to questions, but actually create content for you. Instead of the functional but still somewhat awkward vernacular of search engine technology, where you have to dive down a rabbit's warren of links in order to extract meaning and substance, ChatGPT does the heavy lifting for you. ChatGPT can write software code or an essay in response to a prompt from a business school professor in the blink of an eye.

Created by Silicon Valley phenomena OpenAI, ChatGPT has been the most successful new consumer technology launch in history. As AI angel investor Allie K. Miller noted in a LinkedIn post, it took Netflix about three and a half years to reach 1 million users, while ChatGPT got there in five days after its launch in late November 2022.[1] The service reached 100 million users in under two months.[2] It has become ubiquitous in both campus and company settings, changing how people learn and work.

Back to our impromptu meeting in the winter of 2023. Some professors struggled with the implications of this AI tool. Test preparation company Chegg saw its stock price plummet 48 percent in a single day when the CEO described the impact of ChatGPT on his forward projections. IBM announced a halt on new hiring and Samsung stated it would ban the technology.[3]

The theory and practice of creating AI innovation, which is the substance of the Imperial College "AI Ventures" class, suddenly became very personal as these disruptions began to roil higher education. My two faculty colleagues, Chris Tucci and Yves-Alexandre de Montjoye, and I had constructed a curriculum that provided carefully wrought scaffolding to help our mix of business and computing students to architect a new enterprise in the AI domain. A series of written assignments prompted students to assemble components of their business plans, which they would then present at the end of the module.

Normally this sort of work entails a reasonable amount of time to think through, research competition and market, and articulate a cogent set of activities around launching the new venture. Now, thanks to ChatGPT, students can complete the assignment in five minutes instead of five weeks. We had to come up with a new approach because it appeared inevitable that students would avail themselves of ChatGPT in completing their assignments.

Dean Veloso suggested to me that we try the critical thinking approach to how we design our assessments. And so off we went, retooling an entire curriculum in a week.

What we came out with at the end of this condensed process was a decision to explicitly require the students to partner with their LLM buddy and tell it to write portions of the business plan. The students then engaged in critical thinking, examining the output from the LLM (usually ChatGPT, but we suggested a dozen alternatives), highlighting what it did well, and explaining what they could do differently in order to make the output usable in their final presentation. Tempted though we were, we did not make use of the generative AI tools for university professors that we uncovered in our research, which can make lesson plans, design assessments, and conduct an array of other tedious, time-consuming tasks associated with creating a detailed curriculum.

We were lucky enough to get an OpenAI executive to come speak to our eighty highly engaged students. While the contents of the discussion are off the record, I can share that it was exciting to be able to expose the class to history as it was being created, a behind-the-scenes look at a new industry being shaped in real time. I couldn't have asked for a better case study. It reminded me of the heady time a few years ago when MIT Professor Alex "Sandy" Pentland, Joost Bonsen, and I created the first graduate financial technology (fintech) class at MIT, bringing in the CEOs who were shaping the headlines and allowing our students direct Q&A about the new world that was opening before them.

Something interesting happened through our learn-by-doing exploration of *generative artificial intelligence* (a topic we will define further in chapter 2). While one student did unearth an important gap in their business strategy using ChatGPT, our students discovered that it has significant limitations. It isn't creative. It tends to repeat itself. It is not yet a complete substitute for a human entrepreneur.

Innovation economist Erik Brynjolfsson at Stanford's Graduate School of Business has argued that the AI revolution will not lead to wholesale jobs displacement, but rather jobs substitution or jobs evolution.[4] In 1965 (or 1865) we didn't have a concept of an "IT help desk specialist" or a "machine learning developer." In this new age of AI, new job specializations are emerging. Five years ago, we didn't have a job called "prompt engineer" (someone who knows how to write queries for LLM systems like ChatGPT). Today, there are dozens of postings on employment websites. David Autor, writing for the National Bureau of Economics Research, notes that "roughly 60 percent of employment [today] is found in job titles that did not exist in 1940."[5] The revolution is at hand.

Erik further argues that true economic expansion will occur when AI systems augment or enhance humans, rather than replace human tasks. We investigate this idea of Human+AI hybrid systems in chapters 6 and 7.

When Bots Attack

Let me not paint an unduly rosy picture of the AI present and future. We've already seen the adverse impact of unregulated AI on society.

Artificial intelligence in concert with human beings has changed the face of the political landscape. But first let's review recent history.

Robotic automation has been reshaping manufacturing for years. The late 1970s brought some of the first large-scale deployments of robots to the factory floor. It contributed to the shift of the British and American manufacturing economies into service economies. What's interesting here is how waves of AI and robotic automation created fundamental changes in each country's society.

First, the machines took jobs away, permanently. Whether in Yorkshire or in the US Rust Belt, in places like Sheffield and

Detroit, a generation of workers was displaced by technology and by globalization. These people were, for all intents and purposes, made permanently unemployed, as their skills weren't transferable and their employers, and society, failed to provide sufficient retraining. For every robot, there is a robot repair person, but those jobs need to be created and workers need to be trained in those new skillsets. During the Brexit vote of 2016, Sheffield, originally expected to vote Remain, shifted to Leave. How did this happen?

Brexiteers might tell you it's because Nigel Farage convincingly campaigned in the region.[6] And without a doubt, he had some influence on the outcome. But something else was going on as well, which helped propel the momentum that he, Boris Johnson, and others pushed.

More than 150,000 social media accounts engaged in Brexit-related activity were linked to Russian intelligence and affiliated entities,[7] which together with Iranian agents generated millions of tweets in support of Leave. It is believed one-third of all Leave tweets in the month immediately prior to the election were generated by bots exhibiting characteristics common of Russian troll-farm activity.[8] Cyber firm F-Secure has tracked continued activity years later in support of Brexit, identifying as many as 18 million suspect tweets in less than two months in 2019.[9] The Russia Report on the attacks, finally released in July 2020 more than a year-and-a-half after it was completed, outlined indisputable evidence of Russian meddling in UK politics, including specifically around the Brexit vote.[10] AI, albeit under the firm control of human hands, was directly responsible for promoting messages that encouraged fear and xenophobia.

Would people have listened as intently if they hadn't for decades felt *left behind*? The anger expressed at the polls was genuine, and came, in part, from people fed up with having no discernible future, many of whom were unemployed and disenfranchised.

The bots would not have been able to swing the elections if it were not for a disaffected, alienated electorate that made both the Brexit vote and the 2016 US presidential election exceedingly close. Without a sense of participation in the economic growth that followed the 2008 recession, without the chance to enjoy wealth creation of the fruits of the European Union, why would these *left-behinders* feel optimistic about the future and positive about the promise of more of the same? Because more of the same was, essentially, the core political platform of both the Remainers in the United Kingdom and the Hillary Clinton campaign in the United States.

By themselves, these disaffected voters were statistically a minority of the voting-age population. But what happened when they were combined with outside influence that suppressed the mildly positive majority and encouraged extremists in the minority? We have witnessed the results, amplified perhaps by the Covid-19 crisis but apparent even without it.

Brexit has sometimes been referred to as the "dress rehearsal" by Russian intelligence for the US presidential election. And indeed, we see proportionate results: in the 2016 US presidential election, more than 40 million "fake news" tweets propagated on Twitter (now called X).[11] A "significant portion" of users were deemed to actually be bots, responsible for between 20 and 25 percent of all of the content.[12] Imagine if one out of every four or five people you talked to was a robot. Imagine if you couldn't tell the difference.

Researchers from the National Bureau of Economic Research estimated that the Leave vote in the United Kingdom during the Brexit referendum was increased 1.76 percent through the actions taken by bots, and Donald Trump's votes in the US presidential election in 2016 were boosted 3.23 percent. Leave won 51.9 percent to 48.11 percent. Trump actually lost the popular vote in the United States, but due to a quirk of how the US presidential system works (the Electoral College), his wins in strategic locales meant he was able to take the White House. The bot swing was within the margin of error of the estimation techniques of the researchers.[13] University of California, Berkeley researcher Yuriy Gorodnichenko and Swansea University researchers Tho Pham and Oleksandr Talavera stated, "Our results suggest that, given narrow margins of victories in each vote, bots' effect was likely marginal but possibly large enough to affect the outcomes."

You're not paranoid if they're actually out to get you. The bots attacked, and they continue to do so.

AI Head Meddling

How could we have arrived at a point where millions of people may have had their votes swayed in national elections? It's enough to make you depressed. Let's consult a psychiatrist.

"I'll be your therapist today."

"I feel sad."

"Tell me more about such feelings."

"My children never call me."

"What does that suggest to you?"

By now, you have probably figured out that this is a primitive AI. In the mid-1960s, when MIT researcher Joseph Weizenbaum first put the DOCTOR script into the ELIZA expert system, it was a revolutionary moment in computer science. This was the first chatbot that successfully impersonated a real person, passing what's known as the Turing Test. If you're curious, you can play with ELIZA yourself at websites like this one: https://web.njit.edu/~ronkowit/eliza.html.

Mathematician and pioneer of computing Alan Turing, who cracked the Enigma code at Bletchley Park to help the Allied forces win the Second World War and who was deemed the father of artificial intelligence,[14] posed a benchmark for the development of AI. He said that if a computer program could be written that could interact in such a manner that someone couldn't tell if they were interacting with a machine or a person, it would pass the first threshold of demonstrating that it's a machine that thinks like a human being. It would, by definition, be classified as *artificial intelligence*. We'll investigate more about the different types of artificial intelligences in the next chapter, but it's worth considering the point that the dawn of AI began with a chatbot.

In modern times, we see chatbots providing customer service on websites, tirelessly, benignly, without ever getting annoyed at dumb questions. We also see them invading dating apps, fronted by repurposed pictures of models or simply stolen images of attractive people, luring us into subscribing to adult websites or, more malignly, conning lonely hearts out of hundreds of thousands in savings. The invasion is so prolific it has prompted numerous articles with titles like "How to Tell If You're Talking to a Bot: The Complete Guide to Chatbots" and "Spot the Bot: Keep Bots from Taking Over on Dating Sites," and even a private investigation service offering a piece on "How to Spot Scams & Bots on Tinder and OkCupid." The bots are coming after our bedrooms. The Nigerian prince scam is now interactive.

The origin story of all of these scams was a humble parody of Rogerian therapy (in which the therapist is effectively passive, asking questions that reflect what the client has already said rather initiating new areas of discussion). The first bot was intended to illustrate how inane (in the view of the authors) this particular brand of psychiatry was. Users were absolutely convinced that ELIZA had feelings and could think. Our tendency as a species to anthropomorphize inanimate objects found a new model of expression that synchronized with technology engineered to emulate human beings. Perhaps it was only a matter of time before we would go from pouring our hearts out to an unthinking robot (one that was actually written as a parody of psychiatrists, dumbly parroting back what we said in the form of a series of prompt questions) to simply mistaking political chatbots for actual people—people who think just like we do, even down to the darkest corners of our psyches. But rather than soothe our souls by *listening* to our troubles, these chatbots encouraged polarization to such a degree that society fractured. The foundations of Western democracy grew a bit shakier with these Manchurian chatbots, albeit ones that weren't fully autonomous, but were tuned and contextualized with the aid of human intervention.

Chatbot-enabled electoral polarization didn't happen in a vacuum. Another, more subtle form of artificial intelligence systems had already been working to push people apart in the form of the Facebook feed. People like people who think like them. If you promote this positive feedback loop, you can create an information or behavioral cascade that suddenly gets large numbers of people moving in a certain direction. Demagogues have known this for centuries. With the advent of AI and with the ability to make chatbots that attack, this knowledge can now be made predictable and scalable, with terrible implications for society.

Witness the polarization of the American electorate over the course of about twenty years. Donald Trump did not spring fully formed from the brow of Ronald Reagan. The Trumpists of today would have found Reagan to be a lefty who was hopelessly liberal in their eyes. The Republican Party of the 1980s proudly talked about the "Big Tent" that could encompass many views. They had to—at the time, that was how you won elections, by appealing to the center. What happened to set up the current dynamic, which plays itself out as much in the streets of Birmingham as it does in the hallways of Washington, DC?

Let's look at some numbers that reveal what polarization looks like in the American electorate:

As you can see from figure 1-1, the political leanings of Americans gradually shifted from having a fairly cohesive central mass to separating into increasingly polarized liberal and conservative camps. From 1994 to 2004, despite the fragmentation of media, rancorous political debate and a war in Iraq, Democrats and Republicans were relatively convergent and there was a political center. The blame could not be laid on Fox News, which was founded in 1996. By 2015, the center

FIGURE 1-1

Changes in voter identification patterns, 1994–2015

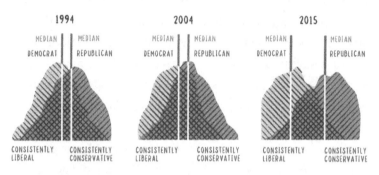

Source: Pew Research Center.

could not hold, and things flew apart. Arguably, things have become even more extreme in the United States since 2015, to such a degree that democratic mayors in large cities were fighting armed invasion and abduction of citizens off the streets by unmarked government vehicles at the instruction of a Republican federal administration.[15]

What happened in 2004, you might wonder? Facebook was founded.

There are some who may criticize me for confusing correlation with causation. I am not alone in my contention that, by legitimizing fringe extremist sources, AI newsfeed algorithms and unconstrained chatbots were directly responsible for electoral polarization.[16]

Facebook makes money through selling advertising, which is driven by how many people look at the website and interact with its content. Through AI analysis of our behavior, Facebook discovered that more extreme headlines give us a little thrill. When we get that charge, we stay on the site longer and we click more—particularly on extreme articles that agree with our intrinsic biases. Generally speaking, Facebook doesn't care about Democrat or Republican, liberal or conservative.[17] Facebook cares about making money. More page views and more time on site means more profit.

Chatbots were weaponized and gleefully deployed into the fertile environment created by Facebook and other receptive social media in both the United Kingdom and the United States (and to a lesser degree in France and other places).[18] They supported far-right extremists and far-left extremists. Anything to break the political discourse. Intelligence agencies and government committees have pointed to Russia, Iran, and North Korea as sources of a number of attacks, including use of weaponized chatbots and other attack vectors, up to and including a series of hacks surrounding the 2020 US presidential election.[19] One analyst group called these "weapons of mass distraction."[20]

Chatbots do strange things when they are left unsupervised. Technology titan Microsoft suffered a bit of a public relations disaster in 2016 when it launched AI chatbot Tay. Digesting masses of data from the app formerly known as Twitter, Tay rapidly taught itself to be both racist and sexist. Microsoft pulled it down within sixteen hours of launch.[21] If a simple chatbot can so quickly go off course in an unsupervised learning environment, what might happen with a more sophisticated artificial intelligence in a mere few years, one that is tied to critical systems? What if our self-driving car decided that it would be happier without some smelly human ordering it around?

In a way, we are fortunate that chatbots are so dumb. Yes, they were used to attack democratic systems. They were noticeably machinelike, however, and so researchers and security professionals have been able to identify them. We may soon reach a point in artificial intelligence systems development where we see—or rather don't see—imperceptible AI, invisible AI systems that convincingly create video and audio simulations of people that are so accurate they are impossible to tell apart from the real thing. Then we can really start worrying about what happens when bots attack.

Perhaps I ought to be more worried about the simple threat of the AI author and thought leader that can read more than I can, write better than I can, and produce work at a greater speed than I could ever hope to. Is there anything we can do to avert a world of digital twins that displace us from our jobs? Or are we destined to become obsolete, a faint memory in the minds of the beings who created the machines that will replace us as the dominant life form on the planet? How far away is this grim vision of evil bots from the mirror universe, coming to take over our lives, steal our money, and ruin our reputations?

Thanks to generative AI, we now can easily produce highly realistic *deep fakes*, video and audio that seem as if they were coming from a real person but are actually manufactured by a machine. US President Joe Biden can be made to chant an amusing rap or, more ominously, warn of impending nuclear attack. The risks to society, to the foundations of democracy, have never been greater.

In chapter 9, we'll discuss some of the emerging policy responses to AI threats.

The Fear Index

Robert Harris wrote a 2011 novel, *The Fear Index*, that played with the idea of AI actively promoting a feedback loop to spiral human fear out of control, creating market disruption that the "evil hedge fund" could take advantage of. The HBO TV series *Westworld* envisioned a war between humans and humanoid machines. Part of the terror arose from machines that were made to look like people, passing imperceptibly for human beings to better infiltrate society, which then was subverted in service of the goals of the machines. Likewise, the *Matrix* movies envisioned technology gone wrong as humanity was turned into mere batteries to power the machine empire, notwithstanding the faulty physics needed to make that possible.[22]

Fear of science and technology is nothing new. When hooligans tear down 5G towers, they act out the same mindless savagery embodied in Mary Shelley's *Frankenstein*, where pitchfork-wielding villagers chase a biological artificial intelligence to its death. Shelley based part of her story on the legend of an alchemist who conducted research at Frankenstein Castle centuries before she traveled through the region along the Rhine, which likely helped inspire her to write her opus.[23] One could trace influences on her, in turn, back to the legends of the Golem predating 1100 and forward to the Isaac Asimov robot novels of the 1950s where he envisioned a set of laws programmed into machines so they wouldn't harm humanity. This utopian vision of robotic safety was undermined in more recent films such as *Her* and *Ex Machina*. Boy meets girl robot. Boy falls in love with girl robot. Girl robot abandons boy and terrorizes society.

AI, among all technologies, seems to have a special ability to inspire fear, particularly in Western Europe and the United States. We rarely, if ever, see movies or books about the dangers of quantum teleportation, or headlines about politicians and workers railing about lithium batteries exploding. Our imaginations are captured by images of machines running amok, of killer robots and disposable humanity.

Partially, this fear may come from the way in which we have welcomed AI into our lives. We have taken AI onto our phones and use it to navigate or to shop. We have taken AI into our homes and use it to provide entertainment—either explicitly, when we ask Alexa to play us music, or implicitly, when we allow Netflix to recommend a movie to us. It's everywhere. Some people have taken to putting sexy or soothing voices on to their in-home AI interfaces, and have a machine read poetry or erotic literature to them. Or a bedtime story.

And we rely on AI, increasingly, to tell us what is what. This embeds a new kind of danger when the AI begins deviating from normative reality.

Hallucinations

An AI hallucination is an expression of artificial intelligence going *off the rails*. Specifically, it means that the AI is doing things that it was not trained to do—so much so that it enters into a kind of delusional state and begins making things up.

For example, let's say you teach an artificial intelligence to speak colloquial language and it starts spewing nonsense.

Meta describes it as when "a bot confidently says something that is not true."[24]

This reveals an important and fundamental characteristic of artificial intelligence: its lack of reliability.

Thanks to popular culture, we are given to thinking that artificial intelligence is either predictable or in its own mind rational. So, for example, the artificial intelligence in *2001: A Space Odyssey* attacking the crew because it was given bad programming by humans. There's a rational explanation for why the AI stopped doing what it was supposed to be doing and started killing people. It did so because people messed it up with conflicting instructions. The AI was trained to pursue truth and honesty, and then people told it to lie.

AIs are actually a great deal more complicated and less predictable than how they appear in media. Some of the most powerful approaches to AI deliberately and directly design systems based on the architecture of the human brain. The AI has layers upon layers of linked networks, similar to how the human brain is composed of linked networks of neurons. This layered approach of neural networks can make AI extremely powerful. This is how ChatGPT works—what's referred to as an LLM built in a deep learning system.

It shouldn't surprise anyone, then, that the AI misbehaving looks a bit like the human brain misbehaving. And so we use a psychological term to describe this erroneous behavior: hallucinations.

Because ChatGPT and similar large language systems build sentences based on relationships of prior words, the longer the piece you ask them to write, the greater the chance they will spiral off into some really odd directions. However, if you iterate with the AI, a domain space sometimes called *prompt engineering* (as we will discuss further in chapter 7), you can refine the outputs and get significantly better answers.

We continue to research, and train our AI researchers, on dealing with model management, model drift, and systems design. For example, there was a major paper a few years ago on the concept of *underspecification*—essentially, you train AI on one set of data and it gives you good results, so you deploy it; but then it encounters the real world, and you discover that the training data wasn't representative of real-world conditions, meaning that the answers the model gives you are at best useless, and at worst harmful.[25]

AI hallucinations are another source of AI error, one that is still poorly understood by expert AI researchers and remains an area of intense study—one that needs more funding; AI is still very much an emergent technology, eighty years after we built the first AI during the Second World War. With AI hallucinations, the AI will not only make up fake facts; it will even fabricate citations (fake scientific articles) in order to support its delusion. This might include clever fakes: actual authors and real scientific journals, but fictitious articles. *Caveat emptor*, indeed.

What this means, in practical terms, is that we should be very wary of undue reliance on generative AI to the exclusion of human involvement.

Let's take a minute to look at what the different kinds of artificial intelligence are and where the state of the art stands today. That's the subject of our next chapter.

Chapter 1: The Rundown

- Developing a strategy to understand and respond to AI has never been more urgent, due to the rise of generative AIs like ChatGPT.

- AI has already had global-scale impact on society in the past decade, and more change is coming.

- The first AI to fool humans into believing it could think (passing the Turing test) was invented in 1965. They have only become more sophisticated since then.

- It's important to understand AI, because it is more complicated and less predictable than how it is depicted in the media.

2

Defining AI

Understanding Terminology

Chapter 2: What You Need to Know

- Categories of AI include expert systems, machine learning, deep learning, generative AI, and artificial general intelligence (AGI).

- Dimensions to consider include structured versus instructed data, and supervised versus unsupervised learning.

- Human+AI systems open up new potential for societal and economic advancement.

It can seem, to the layperson, that there's a bewildering array of terminology that gets used in the description of artificial intelligence. It's important to understand the different kinds of AI because that can help reveal the threats, and opportunities, that AI systems present.

We're going to understand in this chapter, in relatively nontechnical language, the bestiary of artificial intelligence. Better to think of it as an unarmed safari than a trip to the zoo, because some of these AIs pose a very real threat to your future livelihood. Others, on the other hand, could represent utopia. While the early chapters of this book, including this one, generally paint a grim view of the next ten to twenty years, I encourage you to recall that once Pandora let loose all of the ills on the world, what remained was Hope.

Expert Systems

Rules-based expert systems and other kinds of rules-based computer systems were some of the earliest AIs. "If A, then B" is the central programming concept. You get a smart human to imagine all of the possible answers to a set of questions or circumstances, or perhaps you create clever mimicry in the case of ELIZA and newer generation rules-based chatbots. The machine is following a big set of rules that deterministically drives its actions: if a certain circumstance is presented, take one action; if another circumstance is presented, take another, and so on.

The reason most chatbots today seem dumb is because they are. They qualify as artificial intelligence by the most basic instance of the definition. An important myth to puncture is the notion that *artificial intelligence* is automatically smarter than humans. Chatbots are typically following a variation of a table of rules, sometimes randomly accessed (such as in the case of some Tinder scambots), sometimes tied directly to a discrete set of answers like in an online help system. Often minimally programmed, they are as limited as their list of answers to specific phrases or words. I would argue that the reason ELIZA worked better than expected by its creator is that it was put into a very specific context, the therapy conversation, and it was mimicking a very specific type of therapy, Rogerian, which consists of asking questions back to the patient following a near-formulistic model. ELIZA has been the inspiration of many of today's modern chatbots, at least in spirit, but chatbots that use this model are only as good as the particular programming (and programmers) involved. It is possible to manufacture smarter chatbots, as we will learn in chapter 8, but many of today's chatbots are primitive and rules based.

More serious expert systems have considerably more investment placed into them, but nonetheless follow the same principles of a programmed set of rules that trigger specific actions or results based on specific inputs. The catch is that programmers have to spend quite a bit of time in a structured capture process, gleaning information from experts in order to program an expert system. This, in turn, limits the applicability of these types of AI. Research on the performance of expert systems shows that their effectiveness is influenced by such factors as the narrowness of the questions being answered, the manner in which the information architecture is designed, and the people involved (both expert and programmer). The type of knowledge itself limits the viability of the expert system.[1]

What would be a viable expert system, versus a novelty? One example would be configuring computer hardware and software.[2] This used to be a task that needed extensive manual labor by a highly trained IT professional. It is, however, a constrained system: there are only so many types of computers, and only so many possible combinations of hardware and software. This is a dynamic that lends itself to codifying a taxonomy of rules and specific scenarios; if faced with system X, then make software perform function Y.

While posing a modest threat to the livelihood of the IT department, a second-order effect of removing the direct intervention of a highly trained, on-site IT professional was that it made it more feasible to move IT functions offsite, and eventually even offshore: AI-enabled labor disruption twinned with the trend of globalization. The downstream effects have been profound in many ways. In 2017, I was one of the 20,000 passengers caught up in the mess when the entire British Airways computer system went down across the globe. Stranded at Heathrow, I was fighting to get across the Atlantic so I could give a speech to the central bank of Chile. Air Canada eventually rescued me. It turned out that outsourcing British Airways' IT function was not perhaps the best systems reliability strategy.[3] I was given to understand that a poorly trained outsourced systems engineer mishandled some critical power systems, and because they had fired the internal British Airways IT people who knew how to handle the problem, there was no one to call. They essentially broke the on/off switch. Prophetically, British Airways had another notable IT failure while I was attempting to finish this writing book, canceling my flight out of Mumbai in the middle of the night.

What if you run into complex systems? What if you aren't sure what you need to do with a different set of circumstances? Expert systems definitionally rely on frameworks that can fit within the scope of the human mind. What if you are faced with gigantic amounts of data that defy the span of human cognition? The limitations of expert systems, coupled with growing compute power, the plummeting cost of memory, and the accelerating pace of data created or captured by sensors and sensing platforms large and small, led to the emergence of another form of artificial intelligence: machine learning.

Machine Learning

Machine learning is a more sophisticated form of artificial intelligence than expert systems. Machine learning programs learn from data and tend to get more accurate as you feed them more data. When I say "more data," I mean very large quantities of data. It is perhaps no coincidence that machine learning systems really began to come into their own within the past ten to fifteen years, as the quantities of data generated from internet usage—from satellites, from wearable computers, from mobile communication networks, and other sources—started to achieve truly massive volumes.

Let's pretend it's 2014, and you are building a new facial recognition system using machine learning. With a limited dataset, you can get to about 96 percent accuracy. Great. It still means that one time out of twenty it's going to get it wrong. Thanks to the masses of data being pummeled through facial recognition systems, by 2023 the accuracy rate is now closer to 99.9 percent.[4]

One of the issues is that the system needs to be able to deal with data variety. The difference between 2014 and 2023 is that enough images have been fed through machine learning algorithms that they are now much better at dealing with so-called *edge conditions*—those rare events that only show up occasionally but are enough to mess up your entire model. For example, if you have trained your model only on people without beards, or only white people with beards, your system might struggle with someone who has a different skin tone or facial hair. If your model never encountered close family members that resembled one another, it might never learn how to tell siblings apart.

This concept of edge conditions runs throughout computer modeling; it is not limited to facial recognition. Steve Wozniak is a centimillionaire, but when his wife applied for a credit card, she was purportedly given a credit limit ten times lower than him, as the system had no concept of how to contemplate a wealthy person's wife.[5] In the 2008 financial crisis, and when the Long-Term Capital Management (LTCM) hedge funds collapsed a decade earlier, computer models were confronted with so-called black swan events that cascaded through markets and triggered catastrophic losses.

This same concept holds true for teaching machines to translate words that humans express verbally into data, to help cars drive themselves, and to enable a SpaceX rocket to land itself in an upright position. Billions of data points are fed into a system that identifies similarities among sections of data and the machine learning system begins to get better at predicting where the next piece of data should go. If the system doesn't have a big enough dataset that shows it very rare outlier events, it can struggle and sometimes fail. For example, in 2016 an earlier version of the Tesla Autopilot system caused its first driver fatality when the computer got confused by bright sunlight reflecting off the side of a white van and failed to avoid a traffic collision.[6]

We see this everywhere in our daily lives now. Whether it's Netflix recommending a TV show we would like, or

Alexa being able to understand our food order, machine learning systems have permeated popular consumer digital applications.

Another breakthrough in the machine learning era was the aforementioned publication of TensorFlow by Google in 2015. The magic that is derived from trillions of searches that have been run through Google has been reduced to a computer software package, which Google then made freely available. TensorFlow democratized access to powerful, fast machine learning capabilities.

Structured versus Unstructured Data

Data is the water that makes the wheel of AI turn. An example of structured data would be date, time, and GPS coordinates. An example of unstructured data is the words that make up this book, or the pixels that go into a digital photograph or video. Expert systems require highly structured data. Machine learning systems can work with either unstructured or structured data but tend to do better when they are fed preprocessed data, where some structure is applied to help clean up the noise of the original dataset.

Unstructured data is, by definition, data points that don't have much or any relationship to each other. Think about a photograph of a rose. The fact that one pixel is red has little to no bearing on whether or not the next pixel is red, or black, or some other color. The key here is *little*—photo-processing algorithms are smart enough to figure out that, "Hey, that cluster of pixels is all red, so we can use math to describe the shape of the cluster and attach the color red, instead of needing to individually describe each pixel." Now we're starting to put some preprocessing or structure on to what is still fundamentally unstructured data.

Let's look at customer reviews on a website:

"I found this product to be brutal, tasteless, and short."

"I loved my gizmo, it was tremendous."

"Nice."

"Worth the investment."

I made these up, but they're not dissimilar to what you could find on Amazon reviews, on Airbnb, on OpenTable, or a host of other websites that incorporate user reviews into their service offerings. Tweets would be another example of unstructured data that might impact a company marketing a consumer product.

You could pay a marketing analyst to sift through thousands or millions of these kinds of free-form text entries and try to come up with a tabulation of how many positive, neutral, or negative comments there are—information that could help a company run its business better and spot emerging trends. Or you could try to program an expert system on every variation of words and word combinations and assign a value to each of them. You will run into a problem in that instance: How do you teach a computer sarcasm?

Or you could use a machine learning system to parse through masses of data and begin to notice associations. Perhaps you nudge it a bit so that it understands that a particular grouping of comments is *negative*, another is *neutral*, and another is *positive*. As it encounters new comments, the machine can begin classifying into these buckets and teaching itself where to put a new phrase that it hasn't encountered before.

Supervised versus Unsupervised Learning

Machine learning can either occur in a supervised fashion, meaning a human being is keeping a close eye on the systems and models and adjusting them as needed, or in an unsupervised manner, where the computer is teaching itself.

In the example I gave above about customer reviews, I was suggesting a supervised learning model. I, or a marketing manager, or some other human, would take a look at the associations that the system was making, and we would course-correct it, providing *supervision*. We might be able to replace the marketing analyst, but we have to pay a data scientist (who makes two or three times as much money) to review, interpret, and guide the systems. On the other hand, the company can now do things that it simply couldn't do in a cost-effective manner before.

Unsupervised learning is often used in cluster analysis.[7] If you are confronted with a pile of data and you're not sure exactly what you are looking for, or what might be derived from it, you might try using unsupervised learning. Letting the machine sort through the information and identify patterns that exceed the grasp of human cognition can reveal unexpected insights. This could help a vaccine researcher discover a new drug, or help a self-driving car avoid an accident even when encountering an unknown situation.

Let's try a very simple example illustrating the potential of unsupervised learning.

Take this sentence that have just written.

You might have looked at the sentence above and puzzled what I meant. Your brain might have mentally inserted the word "I" before the word "have." Either way, you generally know what I was attempting to communicate even if you have never encountered that particular sentence before. An expert system would halt and catch fire at this sentence, metaphorically speaking at least. An unsupervised learning system might have enough abstraction about meaning and sentence construction that it would be able to derive what I meant even though the sentence is missing "I" in the second half.

This is a transcendent capability. It also creates threats to the job safety of editors and copywriters. It puts at risk the truck driver making $100,000. Advancements in machine learning such as unsupervised learning and deep learning accelerate the potential jobs displacement created by the artificial intelligence economy.

Neural Networks and Deep Learning

The concept of neural networks has been around for years. The idea was that if we replace neurons with transistors and tie them together in a complex pattern that mimics the way neurons connect to each other in the brain, we can replicate human thought. When I was a first-year university student, my independent study project consisted of programming a computer that simulated the performance of a neural network. It was a cool idea, but with the systems at the time it was fairly useless. Neural networks had a fallow period for three decades where the much-heralded promise of artificial intelligence remained elusively out of reach.

They enjoyed a resurgence in recent years as AI technology made new strides in the era of cheap computing power and high-density networks generating sufficiently large volumes of data. Just as the human brain has many layers of neurons connected to each other in a three-dimensional structure, deep learning derives its name from the fact that there are many layers of neural networks tied together.[8]

As you can see in figure 2-1, the more data that you pour into a conventional AI learning system, the better it performs—up to a point. Then it plateaus. Deep learning systems, on the other hand, continuously improve with larger datasets. This diagram illustrates the profound paradigm shift that deep learning delivered to the AI world. Deep learning systems have a significant performance advantage over conventional machine learning. For many applications of machine learning, the pace of improvement of the accuracy of the models—to recognize images, to decipher words, to understand biological structures—was dizzying, but then they would frequently hit a plateau of performance. Even if you poured more data into the machine learning system, it would not appreciably improve past that threshold point. With deep learning systems, endlessly hungry for data, there's no plateau. The more data you put into one, the better it gets.[9]

FIGURE 2-1

Why deep learning

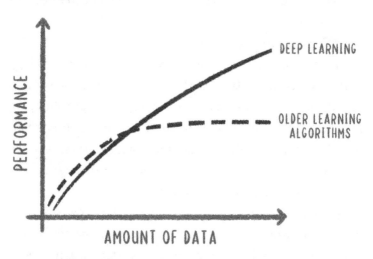

Source: Kumar & Manash, 2019.

Deep learning systems are being deployed with vigor in relation to problem spaces such as language, autonomous vehicles, and financial fraud detection. Your Zoom videoconference call of the future could take speech and translate it automatically into any language while the call is happening, at least if the Chinese technology company Baidu has anything to say about it. The promise of Douglas Adams's Babel fish or the *Star Trek* Universal Translator could finally be fulfilled.[10] United Nations translators may soon need to look for a different line of work.

Despite the multitude of advances made by such systems, they are still relatively specialized. We have not yet reached the ability to create a machine that truly thinks independently and is capable of a range of diverse tasks and ideas. We don't yet have AI systems that can truly be creative. However, with the emergence of generative artificial intelligence (generative AI), we're getting much closer.

Generative AI

Generative AI is a type of artificial intelligence that is able to generate new content using the provision by a user of inputs that could consist of text, pictures, audio, or other data.

It is a probabilistic system that looks at interconnections. For example, if you're modifying an image, such as a photo, it looks at a massive library of prior photos and then determines, for example, if it sees a white pixel (a measure of the smallest element of the photo), what's the likelihood that the next pixel adjacent to that pixel is going to be white, gray, black, or some other color. This very simple concept turns out to be incredibly powerful when applied in practice. It can be used to construct entire new photos, as well as essays, novels, computer code, deepfake voice files, and more.

Computer scientist Stephen Wolfram has provided an excellent analysis of how generative AI systems like ChatGPT work, which is beyond the scope of this book. If you're interested in the detail, I highly recommend you read his post "What Is ChatGPT Doing . . . and Why Does It Work?"[11]

At a high level, he explains the concepts behind the functioning of ChatGPT (built on a large language model called GPT-4 as of this writing, although GPT-5 is already under development, and I'm sure GPT-6 can't be far behind). The user gives the AI a prompt, perhaps a sentence or a few sentences, perhaps more. The AI then begins painstakingly elaborating on this prompt. If it's language based (perhaps the user has asked the AI to write a story), ChatGPT will look at a word, and then look in its massive library to see how commonly another word appears next to that word. If you give the AI the prompt "The boy runs . . . ," the AI might have a series of choices of what comes next: "quickly," "away," "toward," and so on. Word by word, sentence by sentence, paragraph by paragraph, the AI system laboriously constructs meaning. I say "laboriously" because these large language models are computationally (and monetarily) expensive.

ChatGPT can also write computer code, which has resulted in a dramatic acceleration in the potential pace of software development. Other generative AI systems like Midjourney have been producing fantastical images that don't exist in reality but are readily fabricated by AI. Today, generative AI tends to be pretty good at summarizing a large volume of input provided to it, but it's not so good at creative tasks.

Artificial General Intelligence

General artificial intelligence and AGI are two ways of describing the same thing; it is a system where the machine is capable of thinking just like a human. People sometimes also talk about *strong AI*. The varying language is indicative of the nascent character of the field. One fact that many hard-core computer scientists agree on is that AGI is still several years away—perhaps hundreds of years in the view of Oxford machine learning expert Stephen Roberts when I queried him. However, OpenAI claims, today, that it has achieved AGI. It's difficult to verify the claim because, as OpenAI executives have said to me, they've only released a tiny fraction of what they've created.

Even when confronted with an unknown situation, in almost any domain, AGI will be able to respond to it. Because it's totally flexible, AGI would replace the multitude of narrower AI systems we rely on today. It would do an array of tasks better than people.[12] If it existed, it would make large portions of the current labor economy obsolete. We as a species might have more leisure time, or we could see the creation of a vast underclass that is made permanently useless.

University of Oxford's Nick Bostrom points out that if we do succeed in making an AI as smart as a human being, there is no guarantee that it will automatically have human concepts of justice, mercy, or compassion.[13] We may create what we would judge in human terms as a digital psychopath, completely devoid of remorse or regret as it displaces swathes of the job market and eventually wipes out humanity. By its own standards, the AI might be behaving rationally.

Others, such as Luciano Floridi of the Oxford Internet Institute, have proposed a framework of principles that are embedded into the design of AI, so that they are created with a concept of justice and fairness in their very code.[14] However, that vision of AI ethics is threatened by another set of advances in AI: artificial intelligence systems that are created by other artificial intelligence systems. Once the machines start creating improved machines, the risk that we lose control of the outcomes could increase dramatically.

Should the ultimate goal of artificial intelligence research be the creation of AGI? Or should our efforts be directed toward augmenting human intelligence, and exploring the realms of innovation that can forward the needs of human society?

Conversational AI

Conversational AI is an interface layer and system of AI that draws heavily on the realms of deep learning and sometimes generative AI and AGI. With conversational AI, you don't need to be a software developer in order to be able to interact with AI. You can simply describe a problem or query it, and it will elaborate on your idea and give you several sentences, or a page, or several pages, or an entire document.

Primitive versions of conversational AI showed up in our lives at scale as Siri and Amazon Echo. You needed to speak with a certain vernacular ("Siri, play classical music"), but you could talk out loud to the computer instead of having to press buttons or type.

The next generation (whether spoken out loud or typed) of conversational AI systems shows up in the ChatGPT interface, where you speak to the computer as if you were talking to a human being. Describe a problem or a question, and ChatGPT (or Bard, Google's generative AI version, or one of dozens of others now springing up) will give you answers. No less august an authority than Bill Gates has cited one such conversational AI system, from a low-key startup named Inflection, as the potential big winner in the future. While he hopes that Microsoft will win the battle, Mr. Gates has hedged his bets with a company cofounded by Reid Hoffman (LinkedIn), Mustafa

Suleyman (DeepMind), and others. Inflection hopes to be a real-world implementation of a helpful AI assistant similar to JARVIS in Marvel's *Iron Man* movies.[15]

The Environmental Cost of AI

One area that tends to be overlooked is the substantial energy cost of artificial intelligence. OpenAI of San Francisco demonstrated a system that could solve a Rubik's Cube through control of a robot arm. It was a fiendishly difficult AI computation task—one that *Wired* reported probably consumed 2.8 GWh of electricity, or about what you get from three nuclear reactors running for a month.[16] To power all the data centers in the world, we would need 2.5 million wind turbines. We don't have them, of course, which means we're burning fossil fuels (in combination with some other sources, including renewables) in order to harvest the benefits of all of the AI we use today . . . much less what we will be using tomorrow.[17] Deep learning is energy intensive, and we are adding to the world's substantial environmental debt with its carbon footprint.

Human+AI Hybrid Systems

Having covered the role that people can play in making machines smarter, how can machines make people smarter? While we explore this idea more thoroughly in chapter 8, I will briefly touch on it here to contextualize how Human+AI systems fit into the overall taxonomy of artificial intelligence.

One of the simpler Human+AI systems is the Mechanical Turk.

The original Mechanical Turk was demonstrated in 1770 at the court of Archduchess Maria Theresa of Hapsburg. It was a chess game where you, a human, would play against what appeared to be a smart machine that could move the pieces by itself. The inventor, Wolfgang von Kempelen, would go through an elaborate demonstration before the chess game would begin, opening various drawers and cabinets and showing the clockwork housed within. Atop this was a wooden dummy carved to resemble a Turkish man. It was revealed that there was a human chess-playing operator hidden inside the machine who was actually doing the work to make it appear as if the chessboard was autonomously playing against you.[18]

Flash forward to the modern era. Trying to train computers to understand visual imagery has proven to be one of the more complex areas of computer science. However, some very clever chaps at Carnegie Mellon University gave thought to the problem, and also to the dual facts that computers were getting increasingly networked and that usage of the internet was exploding. They realized that they could turn these armies of individuals into a machine for sifting through millions of images, for example, to better train AI on image recognition. Thus reCAPTCHA was born, and was quickly vacuumed up by Google to help the Google AI get smarter.[19]

One clever bit is that the system is also used to provide website security to—ha!—ward off invasions by bots. Only humans are smart enough, right now, to usefully decipher im-

FIGURE 2-2

Example of a reCAPTCHA image

ages in a certain way; the average bot cannot, and a website is thus able to protect itself from attack by armies of dumb bots. So, you present a human user with a picture and break it down into squares—let's say a four-by-four grid—and then have them identify which of the squares contains pictures of traffic lights or cars or fire hydrants (figure 2-2).

It's a trivial task for a human being, but one that is quite difficult, today, for most bots and for many AI systems. These kinds of systems also will look at how you interacted with the website before and as you were clicking on the pictures, based on scrolling, time on site, and mouse movement. It's a good way to screen out fake users from real ones. And along the way, in the background, masses of people are training the Google AI to be smarter about how it analyzes images. As of 2019, over 4.5 million websites had embedded reCAPTCHA, delivering more than 100 person-years of labor every single day, labeling and classifying image data. With a few basic assumptions, we can put an economic figure on this use of people to make AI better. The cost of reCAPTCHA is perhaps $0.001 per authentication (according to competitor hCaptcha). The value of an individual image classification or annotation can be $0.03, so you could estimate $21 billion or more in labor arbitrage that Google has extracted by having people train AI for free.[20]

Amazon's version is called Mechanical Turk or MTurk, and it's rentable as a service. Not limited to images, you can put in any kind of repetitive task for bidding, such as deciphering meaning among user interviews or transcribing audio records. Interestingly, Google's YouTube subsidiary has been using MTurk for years to help improve its AI with human intelligence.[21] Amazon accesses a global network of people, and low-cost overseas labor can provide scale for a variety of tasks.

The labor function is interesting. On the one hand, systems like MTurk pay people for tasks, typically less than $1 per human per task. A new revenue stream has been created for people that can be conducted on the side from other work, generating an incremental income stream. On the other hand, a number of these systems that are being trained are then able to displace human activity in areas like photo editing, video or audio curation, advertising, or retail pricing analysis.

Breeding Centaurs

Let us return to the chess discussion. After chess master Gary Kasparov was beaten by IBM's Deep Blue in 1997, he began experimenting with the notion of bringing together humans and machines to do things that neither could do alone. Take an application that you might encounter in your daily life: the weather forecast. Computer weather models are good, up to a point. But they don't produce the best weather forecast. Human insight and human intuition, combined with a good weather model, can improve the prediction significantly—perhaps by 20 percent on a good day.[22] You can notice the difference if you take time to compare purely computer-generated forecasts with those created with humans in the loop, and then map them to what actually happens with the weather.

These *centaur* creations—half human, half machine—hold the potential to unlock heretofore untold heights of human achievement. Before we ascend to such lofty heights, we are finding terrestrial applications of centaurs. Porsche, for example, is using them to optimize manufacturing processes, combining the fine-tuned ear of an operations engineer with acoustic sampling and modeling to uncover vibration-related issues.[23]

Sanjeev Vohra, who previously led a number of Accenture's AI efforts, is intrigued by what could happen with AI in a computer gaming context. What kind of experience might you have if the AI and you were part of a team in competitive play against other AI–human pairings, perhaps in a complex combat simulation or a strategy game? Could your AI teammate help achieve a certain objective in close coordination with you? How could these game-world constructs then be applied to similar ideas of humans and machines together in simulations intended to help with work, political decision-making, or artistic creations? While Vohra is at the cutting edge, the people he in turn looks to for inspiration are those building real-time AI systems where humans and AI interact frequently for common or conflicting objectives, using very fast, very dynamic AI. These AI models are learning how to interact with humans based on the behaviors of those same humans.

Prediction markets are a type of Human+AI system that we will delve into in chapter 6. At a high level, however, you can think of them as a way to use networked systems to gather *collective* human intelligence and put it together in useful ways. The way they work is that a group of people is gathered together (virtually, these days). Each person predicts some future event, like the date of something occurring, the price of stock, or something similar. The predictions are a decent party trick, but they tend to have an error rate that makes them unusable for anything serious. When we bring artificial intelligence into the equation, however, we are starting to find ways to tune these prediction markets and make them very accurate.

Other types of Human+AI systems that we will explore in part III include the AI coach that can improve your day-to-day job performance, and the ability to surface the latent collective intelligence of an entire company or institution to engage in complex tasks. We see a little of this idea in the Mechanical Turk, but emergent systems are inverting the benefit: instead of exploiting masses of people ever-so-slightly in order to help an AI, we can use AI so that human systems are stronger, more versatile, and more nimble.

We may discover, as we experiment with Human+AI capabilities, that we create new forms of society that we can only dimly grasp today. There could be new ways of people interacting with each other, new ways of cooperating and solving problems, new abilities to form mutual understandings, and new capacities to protect the weakest members of the human tribe. Technologies such as irrigation, antibiotics, and electricity created higher standards of living for many people in disparate geographies. Human society was able to thrive and grow thanks to these advances, and a positivistic view on our ability to shape AI would lead us to believe there's a transcendence awaiting us, beguilingly just beyond our current grasp, if we apply AI in the right way.

First, however, we must confront the very real possibility of large-scale unemployment as AI systems create a ripple effect through the global economy. With it we may see social unrest and upheaval increase, not unlike the radical changes that followed the Industrial Revolution in the 1800s and early 1900s. It won't happen overnight, any more than the creation of sophisticated deep learning systems came weeks or months after the first expert system. It does, however, loom large over the next decade. What trends in labor have emerged over the past fifty years that can point us toward what we should expect next?

Chapter 2: The Rundown

- As AI systems get more powerful, they are increasingly able to take over human tasks.

- Data is what fuels AI, and once deep learning systems (which scale with the data provided to them) emerged, there were few practical limits to how powerful AI could grow.

- *Centaurs* are powerful human-in-the-loop hybrids that can conduct activities that neither humans nor AI do as well by themselves.

3

Evolution of AI
Jobs Displacement

How Did We Get Here?

Chapter 3: What You Need to Know

- Prior to generative AI, experts were forecasting up to 50 percent jobs displacement within the next five years, which would disproportionately impact the global South.

- New analysis reflecting generative AI shows 80 percent jobs displacement, with more job categories in developed countries under threat.

- Lessons drawn from prior tech-disruption cycles can prepare us to navigate this one.

To understand what we are facing now with AI disruption, it's important to look at how automated systems have been steadily eroding the stability of the human labor market.

There is no question that automation has been replacing human workers for decades. Beginning with industrial robots in manufacturing sectors like auto or steel, then migrating to professions like travel agent (Expedia), real estate agent

(Redfin), and taxi dispatcher (Uber), we have seen a march toward the obsolescence of large numbers of jobs previously conducted by humans.

The Manufacturing Meltdown

For each robot, more than one person is replaced. Think tank Oxford Economics (no relation to the University of Oxford) has estimated that the impact on developing countries will be even more severe than in developed countries. Take a look at figure 3-1.

It's one thing to hear that manufacturing economies will be disrupted by AI more than services economies. It's quite another to see the visible disparity between lower-income regions experiencing 2.2 jobs lost for each robot added versus higher-

FIGURE 3-1

Change in number of jobs due to one additional robot

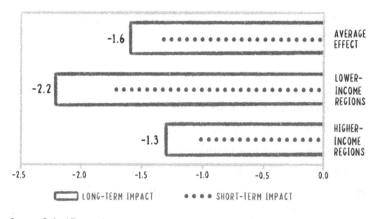

Source: Oxford Economics.

income regions, which have slightly more than a one-for-one replacement. Think about that. In the developed world you have slightly more than a one-for-one replacement rate of people by machines. Conversely, the developing world, already burdened with issues like population growth, insufficient food and water supplies, and inadequate education, is being more severely disrupted by automation than the developed world. It seems a cruel side effect of globalization. First, the most developed countries outsourced their manufacturing and low-skill jobs to the developing nations. Carbon emissions from factories went down in places like the United States and United Kingdom as we exported our pollution-producing industry to China along with the manufacturing jobs that accompanied it. Now with AI and other forms of automation, those lower-skilled manufacturing and service jobs are rapidly being replaced by highly efficient machine systems. The World Economic Forum has suggested that as many as two-thirds of jobs in developing nations could be replaced by automation.

China has noticed. The Chinese government has created national priorities around AI and a coordinated central strategy, which the World Economic Forum has stated will position China to dominate the AI future. China's spending on AI research is more than double that of the United States (expressed as millions of dollars), as you can see illustrated in figure 3-2 (note the rapid ramp-up of Chinese spending on AI versus the relatively stable US figures).

One interesting statistic that Tortoise has identified is that the United Kingdom and Canada (along with Germany) are among the top publishers of AI academic research.

FIGURE 3-2

AI spending, China vs. United States ($bn)

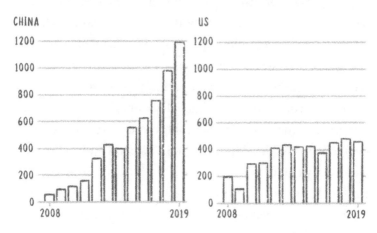

Source: World Economic Forum 2020.

FIGURE 3-3

Number of articles published by top-rated AI experts

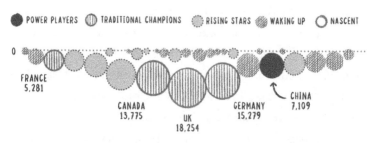

Source: Tortoise Research.

Indeed, both Canada and the United Kingdom have vigorously pursued the AI opportunity. My work with the governments of each country, and in academia in the United Kingdom and United States, has included assisting with the commercialization question: How can we better activate the latent intellectual capital that has so readily been visible in the academic context? What methods will foster innovation ecosystems such that Canadian and British dominance in publications around AI research more effectively make their way into the production of AI commercial applications?

You can see in figure 3-3 that Canada and the United Kingdom (along with Germany) have significant academic productivity in AI research. What steps can we take to better catalyze this effort to realize commercial potential? At the time of writing, I am in the midst of helping to launch an artificial intelligence initiative to help multiple academic institutions create new AI companies out of university research, with an emphasis on *trusted* or *ethical* AI. How can we embed human ethics and morals into AI systems (which of course prompts the question, *whose* ethics and morals?). There is a material benefit to companies that embrace this approach, or at the very least a material diminution of risk—billions of pounds in fines have been levied against companies like HSBC and Meta for violations of regulations covering anti-money laundering and data privacy. AI systems materially increase the risk of more such violations if they are not properly safeguarded.

The challenges before us are daunting and invigorating in equal measure. At its heart, trustworthy and responsible AI (the domain that we are developing in the Trusted AI Alliance) seeks to ensure that the artificial intelligence systems we build and deploy reflect the values of humans. When they make decisions, we want them to make decisions that are legal, moral, and reflective of the ethical code that is relevant to the particular society that is deploying that AI. These values can be quite specific—even within Europe, for example, the United Kingdom has a different perspective on the trade-offs between security and privacy than, say, Germany. The United Kingdom has decided to sacrifice personal liberty in order to construct better security; a web of CCTV cameras was able to identify the terrorists behind the July 7 London bomb attacks within seventy-two hours. Germany, in contrast, has decided to protect privacy, even if it results in a somewhat degraded security posture.

Bridging the Productivity Gap: Working up the Pyramid

As machine systems have become more sophisticated, so too have the kinds of jobs being replaced. Manufacturing positions were among the first to go, but within the past ten years in particular, higher- and higher-value jobs have been replaced (see figure 3-4).

I had the privilege in 2023 of working alongside the research department of Evercore ISI in an effort to better understand the effects that AI was having and is likely to have on the global economy. Evercore, one of the top investment banks in the world, wanted to come up with a novel perspective on separating fact from hype in the AI revolution. The report, *Generative AI: Productivity's Potential, From Macro to Micro*, and the associated AI Impact Navigator are intended to help investors and corporate leaders make better decisions around what AI means for their portfolios and their businesses.[1]

Among other findings, we leaned into the hypothesis that AI could bridge the mysterious recent productivity gap. If we look at the United States as the world's largest economy and assess productivity growth since the Second World War, in 1948–2019 GDP grew 2.2 percent annually. However, if we focus more recently on the period 2005–2019, growth has slowed to 1.4 percent.[2] One hypothesis is that AI might be the answer to boosting prosperity by reigniting growth.

Part of this solution comes through implementation of AI into higher-wage jobs. Indeed, the latest generations of generative AI are hitting the core of the $100,000 salary positions.

FIGURE 3-4

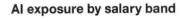

AI exposure by salary band

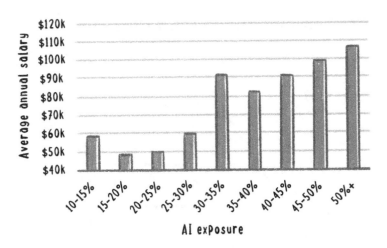

Source: Evercore ISI, 2023.

The rapid replacement of person with machine has created some curious challenges in knowledge-worker industries. For example, let's look at the labor structure of the investment bank (figure 3-5). You could think of this organizational model as a bit of a pyramid scheme. At the bottom are low-paid (per hour) analysts. They scrap among themselves and work ninety-plus-hour weeks, hoping to make their way into the associate pool (perhaps after an MBA). The associates, still numerous but now making a tiny bit more money, are in turn vying for promotion to vice president. The vice presidents are many fewer in number and help to lead teams who do the day-to-day work of engagement.

At the top of the pyramid are the sought-after managing director or partner roles. Captains of the expense-account meal, responsible for an area or book of client businesses, these individuals participate in the profitability of the firm (for the

FIGURE 3-5

Typical investment-banking title progression

sake of this simplified analysis, we'll leave out discussion of executive directors, senior managing directors, assistant vice presidents, etc.).

Part of the system is simply a labor-profitability model: pay an analyst or associate a modest amount of money, charge the client much more, and the partners make money on the difference. The *compensation ratio* of revenue to pay, usually around 50 percent (plus or minus), is a key metric that investors use to evaluate the investment banks that are public.[3]

Another important function of this pyramid model, where one might spend fifteen years going from analyst to partner, is to train up on the culture of the firm, first to embody it, and then to be able to train others in it. For it's not only the simple input–output of hours and spreadsheets that enables Goldman Sachs or Barclays to command a premium rate compared to lesser-known names. The method of working, the way of communicating, the attitude of the banker, these all go into the culture equation. How do you teach culture behaviors to a machine?

Top investment banks readily embraced the use of AI for grunt work typically conducted by analysts, which includes building spreadsheets from piles of data from clients. This seemed a natural evolution of their prior embrace of outsourcing, where this commodity labor was moved from high-cost cities like New York or London to low-cost cities like Mumbai. AI was simply the next evolution in the optimization drive. Every analyst replaced by an AI was another set of profits going directly to the partners.

Suddenly, having cut through the lower ranks of the labor pool, investment banks noticed they had a problem. Who are you going to promote to partner if you've eliminated everyone below you? How will succession be handled? Many of these types of organizations have a pension or retirement plan supported in part by the ongoing activities of the firm: How will that be managed if there's no one left to be promoted? "Last one replaced by AI, turn off the lights!" The phrase assumes a certain macabre predictivity in this instance. I spoke to one major investment bank recently, a firm that consistently ranks top ten in the world. By my estimate, they could replace 90 percent of their research department with AI, saving them perhaps as much as $100 million annually. For a variety of reasons, they won't. However, one of their competitors, or future competitors, will.

Accounting firms, management consultancies, and a variety of these *elevator asset* businesses—so called because the assets of the company leave in the elevators every day—are caught in this tension between the need to increase profitability and the confusion over what the future of the firm looks like when AIs have replaced the historical training ground of the next generation of the firm's leaders.

Indeed, Evercore's fundamental analysis found that white-collar jobs involving skills such as mathematical reasoning, number facility, and oral expression (core activities for investment bankers and management consultants, and a major focus for entry-level professionals in these fields) are highly susceptible to AI. By decomposing jobs into individual tasks, comparing these to what activities different kinds of artificial intelligences do well, and then reconstituting them against industries, we can explore exposure to AI (see figures 3-6 and 3-7). We looked at more than 160 million jobs across 800 occupations, breaking them down into fifty-two abilities and

FIGURE 3-6

Job exposure to AI by broad occupation

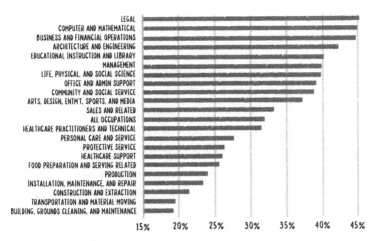

Source: Evercore ISI, 2023.

FIGURE 3-7

Job exposure to AI by industry

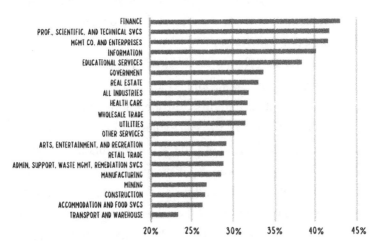

Source: Evercore ISI, 2023.

forty-one tasks. By mapping these against AI proficiencies, we can come up with an exposure mapping.

To review AI impact from a functional perspective, see figure 3-7.

Predicting the Next Target

One interesting approach to anticipate where AI is going to disrupt employment was proposed by Stanford PhD student Michael Webb and elaborated on by the Brookings Institution.[4] Webb suggested that looking at the language of patents and matching it to job descriptions would be a viable means of predicting future AI job disruption.

There is merit to this approach. Patent activity and innovation are viewed by researchers as highly correlated.[5] Typically, there is a window of time between when a patent is filed and when a commercial product or service hits the market, particularly if it's going to be radically disruptive versus simply incremental, so it can be a crystal ball offering a glimpse of the next ten years or so.[6]

So what does Webb, our modern-day Nostradamus, predict with his analysis of patents and AI job disruption? Unsurprisingly, parking lot attendants and locomotive engineers are expected to be hit by AI—these are rules-based activities where sensors and self-driving cars and trains can replace human activity with machine precision. Perhaps less obviously, water treatment plant operators and broadcast equipment operators are also listed by Webb as highly exposed. University professors and podiatrists are least at risk in his model (although he ignores the impact of digital technologies on overall employment in the university realm, which is another conversation). In fact, a colleague of mine from Imperial College, David Lefevre, has mapped out exactly how we can replace eight or nine out of ten university professors with AI. Chemical engineers and optometrists: in danger. Food prep workers and animal caretakers: safe.[7]

But could these ideas actually play out? Let's look at a couple of professions that might less obviously be subject to AI disruption, that once were viewed as stable or safe or reliant on creativity—something machines historically have been bad at.

A Mountain of Debt and a Child's Sand Shovel

A law degree used to be viewed as an automatic ticket to prosperity. In the 1980s pinstripes were glorified. The "white shoe" law partner strode through a city like New York with arrogance and pride. Invest in your legal education, go to a good school. Sure, you may graduate with debt, but you'd be assured of a long career and an easy retirement.

Beneath that person, typically a man, was a pyramid of well-paid but overtaxed associates would churn through billable hours. The unit of production, and profit, was the hallowed billable hour. Charge a client $350 an hour for an associate, pay them about $35 an hour: that labor arbitrage was the engine of profit.

One major source of generating these billable hours was *discovery*, where millions of pages of documents had to be reviewed during the course of a complex case. The intent of discovery was to review the relevant documents and allow each side to make an argument around them.

Artificial intelligence has slowly been chipping away at this bastion of high-value activity where interpretation, not just recognition, is needed. Which document is relevant? What argument might be made about a particular aspect of a case?

First, documents were scanned into the computer and optical character recognition (OCR) was used to convert this information to data and ultimately words. OCR technology has been steadily improving for years. These days, many widely available OCR systems deliver 99 percent or better results when scanning documents,[8] although the rates are lower for things like street signs or other nonstandard surfaces.

Next, we were able to apply semantic analysis to the text. When artificial intelligence was first being developed, we had to rely on rules-based expert systems, which were laborious to program and inflexible. As more-sophisticated forms of artificial intelligence emerged, such as machine learning and deep learning, we began to have machines that could understand meaning and associations—very high-order thinking.

Today, eDiscovery is big business, expected to reach a value of nearly $21 billion by 2024.[9] That market growth is coming at the cost of eliminating manual labor by highly trained humans. No longer are associates with expensive law degrees hunched over piles of documents or peering dimly into computer screens, trying to remember the links between a phrase on page 300 of one document and a paragraph on page 647 of another document. Machine systems effortlessly glide through millions of pages of documents, proposing and discarding potential issues, and only delivering the most relevant information to the human operator for consideration.

And the legal profession is in the middle of a crisis. Academic institutions have been turning out lawyers, but there are fewer and fewer jobs for them to assume. In the United States, the average lawyer graduates with about $142,000 of cumulative debt, and more than 33,000 lawyers graduated in 2019. That's $4.7 billion of indebtedness a year, in a profession that is rapidly being automated.[10] A mountain of debt is piled on to the graduating lawyer, and with decreasing wage-negotiating power, there is a vanishingly small shovel with which to clear it. Prospective law students have noticed. Law school enrollment has been sliding for a decade.[11]

Globally, the legal profession is seeing widespread changes, yet the educational systems supporting them are responding with varying degrees of success. Singapore, never one to let an opportunity to embrace future-facing technology pass it by, has a major initiative in this area of legal educational innovation, trying to make lawyers more conversant with and adept at capitalizing on technology.[12] Various organs of government and education have formally set strategic priorities to incorporate legal pedagogy into undergraduate learning, supported by media campaigns emphasizing the importance of legal education.[13]

Even greater disruptions in the legal profession are brewing. The MIT Computational Law Project, started by Dazza Greenwood and Professor Alex Pentland, aims to "explore the ways that law and legal processes can be reimagined and engineered as computational systems."[14] Their associated activities include hackathons and other idea-expanding platforms to take academic theory and traverse the divide to real-world implementation. Pentland's name is one you will see several times in this book; he and I have collaborated on numerous occasions with a focus on *extended intelligence*, an emerging field of how AI and humans can work together.

The Computational Law Project is convening innovators from a span of academia and practice, exploring topics like how we can automate contracts so that they are not only written by machines (think of a Chart Wizard for legal documents), but can even resolve conflict among themselves. Imagine that—instead of spending large sums of money on litigation or arbitration, two AIs could argue through how to resolve differences in a matter of seconds or minutes. Billable hours, the holiest of holies of the legal profession, will evaporate like water on a hot griddle. It's not all about replacement for efficiency's sake. Greenwood described to me that the process of discovery when he was starting out as a lawyer could be physically dangerous sometimes—young associates would have to navigate dangerous file rooms with haphazardly stacked, heavy boxes of files riddled with spiders, combing through dusty documents for hours when preparing a case. With electronic discovery, particularly when it is enhanced by AI, it has morphed into a faster, safer process. ChatGPT and its competitors like Google Bard and Anthropic.AI stand to take most of the drudgery—and cost—of the legal profession and make it disappear in a cloud of bits and bytes.

The amount of money at stake approaches $1 trillion, which is the expected size of the global legal services market in 2025. That doesn't include the cost of settlements. With this much money in play, it's an obvious place for venture capitalists and entrepreneurs to direct their energies.[15]

You might say, "Why should I care about a few lawyers?"

They're not the only knowledge profession that's being automated. Let's take a look at changes in media and publishing. The story is in some ways worse because the industry had insight that the changes were coming, and did nothing to act on that knowledge.

Media Misguidance

In the early 1980s, legendary futurist Nicholas Negroponte and MIT President Jerome Wiesner foresaw that this new thing that digital technology would enable, something labeled *media*, was going to transform everything. They managed to convince a number of sizable media companies to fund research into this and created the MIT Media Lab. Out of this innovation hotbed a multitude of new technologies emerged that ranged from LEGO Mindstorms and *Guitar Hero* to the E Ink that powers the Amazon Kindle.

The media saw it coming. And they dismissed it.

I was a digital media investor for NBC in the late 1990s. We were pushing the frontiers of how an incumbent industry player responds to technology-driven disruption for a period of time, because NBC had a very forward-looking senior executive name Tom Rogers who built an entire team to pursue new opportunities. We were early investors and adopters of the kinds of technologies that make the internet go today, from edge network systems like Akamai to streaming services like Hulu, the creation and development of which were supported by our investments. Meanwhile our colleagues in the print media world who were trying to help their conglomerates pivot into the digital realm—in everything from magazines to books—struggled. NBC and the other network companies have experienced massive change due to AI and other digital technologies, to be certain, but I will argue that they have held on to more of their economic value than the conventional print media outlets have. If anything, some film and television companies have gone too far, too fast, and adopted AI technology so readily that it has stimulated a backlash in the form of widespread strikes of actors and writers. My former NBC colleague David Zaslav, CEO of Warner Bros. Discovery, has found himself in the middle of this AI automation controversy.[16]

In figure 3-8, look at advertising spend on print versus digital channels like Google, and you will understand why the newspaper industry collapsed.

Newspapers used to make money from those little classified advertisements at the back. The team of advertising specialists who would answer telephones or make outbound calls to car dealerships to convince them to place ads were replaced with automated machine bidding systems. Armies of typesetters and printers' assistants and delivery personnel were replaced with digital systems. Between Google search on the one hand and craigslist on the other, their entire business was decimated, and they reacted too slowly to the changes. Figure 3-8

FIGURE 3-8

Newspaper vs. Google ad sales ($bn)

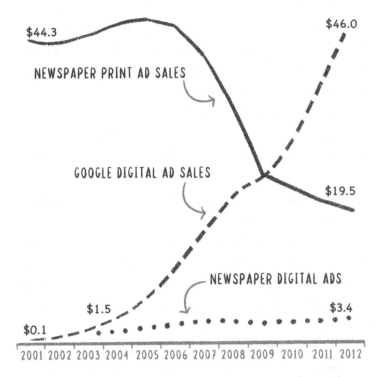

$44.3

NEWSPAPER PRINT AD SALES

$46.0

GOOGLE DIGITAL AD SALES

$19.5

NEWSPAPER DIGITAL ADS

$1.5

$3.4

$0.1

2001 2002 2003 2004 2005 2006 2007 2008 2009 2010 2011 2012

Sources: Newspaper Association of America; Google. Adapted from http://itsheiss.blogspot
.com/2015/03/more-on-slow-but-steady-decline-of.html.

very clearly illustrates the geometric growth of Google's digital ad sales, and with it the precipitous decline of newspaper
print ad sales.

"At least journalists are safe," argued some, pointing out
that a writer could live anywhere and still write and publish
immediately. It was only the advertising teams that were getting upended.

Right?

Perhaps not.

Business press and specialty media saw some of the earliest replacements of human editorial staff with computers. The financial information that public companies need to report every quarter around their revenue and earnings is highly structured data and consistent across different companies. So instead of having a financial reporter read these releases and then write up an article, machines entered the picture to interpret what was happening with the trajectory of a company's financial performance.

More recently, editorial staff has been replaced within Microsoft with artificial intelligence. You see, there's far more news generated every day than there is attention span of news readers to review it. So an editor or team of editors cull the information, talk to their reporters, and decide what appears on the front page, or above the fold, and what might be buried deeper or never published.

That human editorial control is being replaced by AI algorithms. Now machines are deciding what will appear where.

Microsoft is hardly alone in doing this. Facebook's feed is governed by a set of algorithms determining what's going to be more visible for you; someone else will get a completely different set of information. This was not done for various nuanced purposes; they just wanted to make more money.

In fact, quite a bit of research was conducted by Facebook and others on the human brain and what gets you excited. If a company like Facebook shows you something that you like, or that reinforces your existing beliefs, you get a little hit of endorphins. And this makes you want to engage a little more, and you get another hit, and so on. The system of positive reinforcement makes Facebook addictive.

Prior to the coronavirus crisis, the average Facebook user would scroll on their app an amount of content equal to the height of the Statue of Liberty. Under Covid-19 lockdown, according to the Facebook ad team, that figure doubled.[17]

But what happens if you simply let these algorithms evolve and allow the artificial intelligence to decide what information to display and what is acceptable to show to which people? What if you remove humans from the loop?

It turns out that provocative false information is much more exciting than boring old accurate news. More and more people start sharing this provocative information over social networks, and you get what are known as information cascades where false rumors are accelerated by AI. Thus is born *fake news*. Around 2.4 billion people get their news and commentary under the aegis of a Facebook algorithm.

Along with this, real news journalism is fading. Reality simply can't compete with the imagination of conspiracy theorists. And so we have another sector of the economy that is going through widespread disruption, and tens of thousands of people are made redundant. The larger effects on societal opinions and norms of enabling machines to determine the longer-term patterns of opinion and thought held by ever-increasing numbers of people remain to be understood.

A Hint of AI-Enabled Futures

This brings us full circle to the question of career, industry, and the future of work in the face of artificial intelligence disruptions.

One of my former students from MIT, Snejina Zacharia, pursued her Sloan MBA at MIT in order to reorient her career. She had been a management consultant before business school at Gartner, a trends-tracking firm, where she spent time thinking structurally about the future and how technology informs that new reality. While at MIT, she decided to go into the insurance industry. Not, at first blush, what you would automatically think of when evaluating future-forward careers.

However, this woman had a plan. Zacharia identified structural inefficiencies in how insurance was sold in the United States and how AI systems could help make pricing and process more efficient for consumers—at the expense of the human intermediaries, namely the insurance agents. Just as Kayak disintermediated travel brokers to help people find better tickets less expensively, so too Zacharia's company, Insurify, is seeking to leverage similar AI systems to help people find better insurance coverage at a lower cost. Once she had tuned her computer systems around customer analytics and marketing, she succeeded in doubling revenue each year and is well on her way to creating the next fintech unicorn.

Are there any safe havens from AI disruption? Let us now turn our attention to the most vulnerable employment areas, which will be followed by chapters investigating careers that may be more resistant to AI replacement.

Vulnerable Jobs

Researchers at Oxford's Martin School have estimated that 47 percent of US jobs could be replaced by AI by the year 2030. Examining 702 job categories, they found that AI risk is moving from low-skill to high-skill professions, and from repetitive, mindless tasks to those requiring high-order pattern recognition, from so-called mechanical tasks to more elaborate forms of thinking. They feel the best defensive position, the jobs at lowest risk, will be in fields that require creative and social intelligence, something we will discuss further in chapter 6.[18]

Semiskilled and Unskilled Labor

Without question, the areas most vulnerable to AI automation are service jobs, namely semiskilled and unskilled labor. Many different types of service jobs are vulnerable in the AI world. Call centers, for example, have been large labor sinks for a number of years, albeit low-wage ones. They are rapidly being replaced by chatbots. Clerical activities including secretarial services and routine assembly-line work, food and hospitality (including reservation staff), and cleaning staff—these are all vulnerable to replacement by artificial intelligence-driven robots. We can include in this highly vulnerable category much of the transportation and logistics industries. Requiring no sleep and limited breaks for power (perhaps augmented by solar cells to reduce even further how long they need to recharge), an end-to-end network of machines can throw as many as 5 million drivers out of work in the United States alone,[19] perhaps 1.2 million in the United Kingdom (representing 8.3 out of every 10 driving jobs).[20]

The carnage will not be limited there—all of the petrol attendants, café workers, and hoteliers who serve the transportation industry likewise will be out of work. Yes, you will need robot-repair people, but that's now no longer a low-skill or unskilled position.

Let us now delve into the areas with considerably less human involvement in an AI future, those job categories that are among the greatest at risk for AI displacement.

The Uberization of the Workforce

The second-order effects of AI systems are also profound. The fractional economy of Uber, Lyft, Airbnb, and other such companies is powered by AI systems that replace human dispatchers, bookers, and managers. A network of users and service providers is tied together in a two-sided platform, where ratings are accumulated and disseminated. *The Vanishing American Corporation* (2016) by Gerald Davis elaborates on the idea that new-wave tech companies are displacing old-line industrial and retail businesses but with far fewer workers. He gives specific attention to the concept of the Uberized workforce.

Walmart is one of the largest private employers in the world with 2.1 million associates.[21] What if, tomorrow, it fired 100 percent of its workers, and converted them into independent contractors operating on an AI-mediated-and-managed app platform like Uber? When you walk into the store, you as a consumer give a rating to everyone that you encounter. These ratings are then analyzed by an AI and combined with other ergonomic and logistical data such as how quickly an associate stocks shelves to help determine who the lowest overall performers are. The lowest-rated workers are fired each day. From a consumer standpoint, this would provide you with greater transparency on who you are encountering in a store, offer a real-time feedback mechanism, and theoretically improve customer service by incentivizing workers to seek to please you.

The societal implications are profound: worker hours would go down, the opportunity for collective bargaining would be diminished, and the likelihood of employee benefits would decrease for these sole traders who all just happen to work for the same large corporation. It would represent a further disenfranchisement of the working class, and increased profits for Walmart shareholders. This increase in profits would benefit investors in Walmart, which ironically includes large numbers of pension schemes for workers. And it requires no additional technology innovation to implement; this example is based on the technology of today.

In theory, Walmart could do this almost immediately if it had the political will and savvy to fend off the outrage from the public and politicians alike. I'm not advocating it, but as Uber and Lyft have shown with their wholesale destruction of the taxi industry in cities all over the world, there might be a risk to Walmart that if it doesn't do it, Amazon or a new rival will as well. Just as Barnes & Noble, which disrupted small, family-owned bookstores in the 1980s and 1990s, was in turn disrupted into irrelevance by Amazon in the 2000s and 2010s, so too Walmart may find itself painted into a corner. "There but for the grace of capitalism go I." Market forces may require that the giant corporations of today continue to find ways to economize using AI, just to stay competitive.

Analytical Roles

Machines are doing more and more complex math faster and more accurately than people. Adding to this, we see tremendous pressure for so-called *elevator asset* businesses, whether they be accounting or banking, to continue to show profit expansion. You can't simply lower wages or your assets will walk out of the elevators, hence the name, so you need to re-engineer how their job is conducted if you want to continue to grow profit margins.

We discussed the investment banking pool previously and the continued diminution of the analyst ranks. Auditors, too, are top of the list of automatable jobs, along with various kinds of insurance professionals and tax professionals. Hybrid technologies, such as combining AI with distributed ledgers, could result in vast and profound changes for the big four accounting firms of EY, PwC, Deloitte, and KPMG. If you think about the process of audit, or tax, it is a highly repeatable set of activities involving numbers. Disparate datasets need to be compiled, assembled, and compared. Structured rules need to be applied, as well as legal and other regulatory precedent. For more sophisticated matters, a probability needs to be assigned and a determination of risk needs to be made. For example, a certain accounting strategy might technically be legal, but may bring with it an increased risk of triggering an expensive audit. This in turn carries a risk that, if the interpretation by the accounting firm is deemed invalid, the company will need to go through the expense, embarrassment, and market capitalization diminution that accompany a restatement of financial performance.

Tax is an area that is getting some attention from AI and blockchain innovators in part because of the repetitive and analytical nature of the process. Today, large corporations spend millions on compliance with disparate tax regulations and filings in multiple domiciles. In theory, an AI-mediated blockchain system that is endorsed by government could reduce cost and time for compliance to mere minutes or seconds. A government's tax AI could interact directly with a company's tax AI, within certain parameters of inquiry and control, and automate many of the inquiries that today require teams of people and many months of work. While this could save billions of dollars in costs, it also means that those human tax professionals become obsolete. Perhaps a few experts are left to mind the systems, but the armies of individual preparers and structurers become redundant.

Addressing tax avoidance is another reason why AI is appealing to government. It is estimated that more than $200 billion a year of global tax revenue is lost to various forms of corporate tax avoidance.[22] Finding and assessing that money could fuel government programs to support hospitals, schools, roads, and food initiatives.

With tax, there is also the issue of trust. It is estimated by the Organisation for Economic Co-Operation and Development (OECD) and the United Nations Economic Commission for Africa that the cost of tax avoidance in Africa ranges from

$50 billion to $100 billion annually.[23] Complexity of tax forms is a significant driver; according to a World Bank report, it can take 908 hours—one full month—to comply with Nigerian tax regulations.[24] Trust and transparency, it turns out, are major issues driving lost tax revenue. Kenya has been cited as a positive example where implementation of an authenticity labeling system, to help consumers identify counterfeit goods (that presumably pay no tax), has improved tax compliance by 45 percent.[25] Conversely, when asked why they don't pay taxes, many Africans will cite a perception of unfairness, a lack of transparency, and a fear of funds being diverted for corrupt purposes.[26]

AI, coupled to an incorruptible, unchangeable, transparent accounting system, could help deliver a way forward. Complex, opaque forms and processes could be completely or nearly completely automated. And another high-value career for a human that requires years of training becomes a task for a machine.

Anything with Repeatable Processes and Rules

Proofreaders, copyeditors . . . the ranks of the future unemployed are growing with more and more job categories.

AI has led to some interesting discontinuities in the media jobs market. While on the one hand, AI advertising systems like Google have destroyed the conventional newspaper industry and AI article-recommendation engines have replaced many editors, the new AI economy has also empowered independent creators to reach larger audiences and generate more revenue. Mid-tier Twitch streamers can make anywhere from $60,000 to $156,000 per year, and the top streamers can make millions, a figure that dwarfs the $48,581 that Indeed tells me a US journalist makes.[27]

Writing books may not be a protected profession for long. Language, in a sense, has its own rules, and as we will learn in a few chapters even my position as an author may (eventually) be threatened. They have yet to invent an AI that will gamely eat a plasticine-like yellow cheese smeared on a stale cracker and then tell humorous anecdotes to a room full of people before signing books. But my time is coming. We will visit an AI author in chapter 6.

AI Programmers

In a bit of a man-bites-dog situation, the construction of increasingly sophisticated AIs will be taken over by slightly less sophisticated AIs within ten or so years' time, displacing human AI programmers. Google, of course, is at the cutting edge of this field, creating a kind of AI called AutoML that can program itself without human intervention. It was created in response to the challenge of finding enough machine learning programmers, and has a goal of enabling someone with a primary-school educational understanding to be able to create AIs.[28] It is perhaps inevitable that most AI programming will be done in the future by computers, not people, at least in fine detail.

We are seeing the beginnings of this with tools like GitHub Copilot and similar systems that automatically generate code. The conventional wisdom I am hearing from those more technically inclined than me is that you can replace a junior programmer, or ten junior programmers, with GitHub Copilot—but you can't (yet) replace one senior programmer. This may change, and we may see senior programmers go away as well, but meanwhile, the same pipeline issues we discussed in banking are emerging in software. Where are the junior jobs, where someone learns their skills and capabilities to be able to grow into senior jobs?

There are roles involved with the design, support, care, and feeding of AI that will continue to be valuable (and as Erik Brynjolfsson has said to me, "For every robot, there is a robot repairman"), but the jobs dislocation, the disruption required to go from point A in the innovation curve to point B, may result in restless armies of people who can't make the switch and become permanently unemployable. I might amend Erik's phrase: "For every 100 robots, there is one single robot repair person."

Intelligence Solutions

I decided to talk to one of the warriors at the frontline of the AI revolution. An intense, expansive thinker, Sanjeev Vohra lays out a structural and thematic view of what's happening with AI and work, a perspective he honed when leading tens of thousands of consultants in Accenture's applied intelligence unit. He also had a seat on the company's managing committee, giving him perspective across all of Accenture's businesses and clients. I find that he's worth listening to.

Vohra feels we are "just entering into the era of intelligence," a concept that encompasses not only the rise of artificial intelligence, but also the growth of understanding of human intelligence, and the birth of systems that incorporate the best of both AI and human intelligences. In his view, the AI-enabled digital revolutions of the past ten years have been led by native digital businesses like Airbnb or Netflix, that lack the baggage that a Global 2000 company (one of the world's 2000 largest companies) carries with it. The revolution is now starting to pivot to encompass rank-and-file industrial companies, traditional consumer brands, and all other areas of corporate life.

Intelligence wasn't a pressing topic for CEOs until a few years ago, but now it is part of Vohra's active conversations with multiple CEOs. He guides clients on a journey that encourages them to consider the following questions: When you think about how to apply AI in your business, what does *good* look like for your particular company? What kind of outcomes are you hoping to achieve? What impact does it have on your workforce? How do your customers interact differently with you when you have AI intermediating or assisting? What can AI tell you about your competition, and how can you respond differently based on that knowledge?

The touchstone he uses to imagine the impact AI can have at work is the adoption of enterprise resource planning (ERP) software. As Vohra puts it, SAP, which developed the software, "changed the world." The change that occurred in large, old-line companies was radical once the data was transparent, their businesses and silos were connected to each other, and they had a single source of truth about what was happening.

Accenture takes a methodical, structural approach to the way it integrates AI into organizations. It reviews a business, its functions and processes, and identifies roles within it. It then considers how humans and AI can perform these roles and systematically redesigns the business around this analysis. Accenture is not alone in mapping this systematic evolution of the labor force. McKinsey, Deloitte, BCG, and Cognizant, to name just a few of the major consultancies, are giving thought to this question of the role AI will play in the future of work, as are multilateral bodies such as the World Economic Forum and the OECD.

I find it notable that both Accenture and Mastercard, two very different companies, refer to their advanced AI divisions as *Intelligence*, not *Artificial Intelligence*. It's a distinctive erasure of the artificiality. This is an intrinsic, inevitable change. Just as we no longer refer to *digital computers* and now call them *computers*, so too we may move away from calling out *artificial* and look at the technology through a spectrum of intelligence, some of it with less human involvement and some of it with more.

Summing Up

Artificial intelligence is a technology that has been developing for many years and has accelerated its evolution within the past decade. There are many different varieties of artificial intelligences, from the somewhat simplistic rules-based expert systems to the more evolved machine learning and deep learning platforms. International interest has emerged in this equation of AI systems development, with a new arms race emerging between China and the Western economies. The United Kingdom is prominent among G7 countries in its overinvestment in AI relative to its population, but questions remain as to how long this leadership position will last.

With these more sophisticated computer technologies comes the ability to reasonably replace ever-larger segments of the human workforce and of human capabilities. This process is not without its moral hazards in creating large numbers of unemployed humans (who in turn express dissatisfaction at the ballot box), and sometimes not without physical hazards, as we have seen when AI-operated motor vehicles fail. AI automation may have a more severe impact on the manufacturing economies of the developing world, but it doesn't discriminate in its inexorable march up the salary ladder. Even investment bankers, once deemed lords of all they surveyed, are now facing dwindling ranks due to AI automation.

All hope is not lost. There are new possibilities emerging in the AI future that create opportunity for a nimble and forward-thinking knowledge worker of tomorrow.

With AI replacing people in all walks of life, from the assembly-line worker to the journalist, what can you do to avert lifetime unemployment? How can you adapt and thrive in the AI future? In our next chapters in part II, we will explore the kinds of skills you need in order to not just survive, but flourish in an AI-enabled workplace and society. We will start with the fundamentals of cognitive flexibility, and then talk about the kinds of careers that can better position you for the inevitable AI automation wave that is cresting. We will subsequently dive into the territory of what kinds of performance, and what kinds of organizations, can be created when Human+AI hybrid systems are optimized.

Chapter 3: The Rundown

- Analytical and programming jobs are under significant threat, as are professions like law, accounting, and management consulting.

- Creative professions like marketing services, writing, and journalism are also facing new threats.

- Artificial intelligence has become a priority for national interest. Some countries are embracing this more proactively than others.

- Industry leaders have been conceptualizing *intelligence* rather than *artificial intelligence* as a strategic frame.

PART II

PLAYING DEFENSE

Part II helps you navigate the treacherous landscape of AI disruption. We identify the critical skills you will need to acquire to succeed if you are in the workforce already, and we suggest AI-resilient careers of tomorrow.

4

Reskilling and Developing Cognitive Flexibility

Chapter 4: What You Need to Know

- Developing cognitive flexibility is essential to navigating the artificial intelligence future.

- You can apply five principles to enhance your cognitive flexibility: practice, reflection, sustained change, peer learning, and creative exploration.

- You may need to overcome decades of training in the traditional education system to unlock your cognitive flexibility.

Cognitive flexibility is one of the building blocks of acquiring new knowledge and functioning effectively in a dynamic business ecosystem. It's an essential trait that hiring managers increasingly are looking for as the cadence of innovation accelerates and the need to be able to pick up new ideas and bring them into practice becomes ever more urgent. With the changes that artificial intelligence is expected to wreak on industry and society, the nature of what is required of the workforce will change even faster. If you want to stay competitive, and win at work in the age of AI, you need to retrain your brain so that you can learn faster and bring that learning to bear in a context relevant to your workplace.

Unfortunately, the conventional manners in which we are taught are ill-suited to keep up with the accelerating pace at which we are expected to learn new facts and absorb new ideas. Many aspects of the educational system have not changed in substance since about AD 1100.

You have a wise person at the front of the room, delivering information from a prepared text. You have rows and rows of students sitting on uncomfortable, creaky wooden benches, trying to take this word stream and turn it into something they can use. This scene would look no more out of place in a medieval church than it would in a twenty-first-century university auditorium at most of the world's 26,000 or so higher education institutions. Interestingly enough, the University of Oxford was born out of a center of ecclesiastical teaching on the same site about 850 years ago, but has since become renowned for its tutorial system, where two or three students engage in active dialogue with a professor about work they have prepared beforehand.

The way the tutorial works is that you complete an assignment and show up to meet with your tutorial partners and your fellow (your professor). You get feedback on your assignment, discuss a topic, and lead up to the next assignment, which you then work on independently. The tutorial system, also used at Cambridge, incorporates some of the techniques of what is considered best practice based on study of cognitive and neuroscience, but was developed more than 130 years ago.[1] Unfortunately, most universities don't operate that way. It's more cost-efficient to jam 500 students into a large lecture hall and have one instructor at the front broadcasting material. It's more efficient to grade multiple-choice exams than to have the student assessed based on their ability to speak and communicate effectively about their ideas.

The Covid-19 crisis laid bare the limitations of the conventional learning model when, overnight, universities worldwide instantly had to convert into delivering over videoconference. One educator shared with me that she was counseled simply to deliver her standard three-hour lectures on Zoom, and that no other preparation was required. Spoiler alert: it's not going to go well. Another educator shared with me that he feels that students in the back half of the semester, the virtual part, got about 20 percent of the learning value that they should have.

A better way is needed. This chapter will help you begin to understand what is wrong with the old way of doing things, and what the new way looks like. Later in the book, we'll talk about how artificial intelligence is beginning to be used to improve the ability of students to learn and work in small groups, including (in a nifty sleight of meta hand) to learn about artificial intelligence.

The Problem with Education

Our current educational system does a good job of training the creativity and mental agility out of us by punishing those who color outside the lines and rewarding conformity. When we are children, we possess a great deal of cognitive flexibility. We are able to invent and play, creating stories with our friends and imagining new worlds. Then, as we enter conventional education systems, we are trained out of our cognitive flexibility. Almost every major educational system currently extant puts people into rules-driven environments dictating what you learn, how long you learn, how quickly you learn it, and how you spend your day.

To a greater or lesser degree, this extends all the way through our undergraduate educations. It also lines up with graduate education, to such a degree that I often say it takes a couple of years to retrain graduate students for useful employment. I say this only half-facetiously; I have taught a number of graduate students, particularly MBA students, who are exceptional executives and who use the university environment as a carefully calibrated tool to achieve the next step in their careers. I also see many students who get lost in the constructs of academia, who overestimate their market value based on the nature of positive reinforcement they've obtained in a top graduate program, and who then flounder for a couple of years after graduating until they find their footing. All too often I feel that we do our students a disservice by providing theoretical constructs and intellectually interesting ideas, but then failing to connect those to management practice. We reward those students who agree with our epistemologies and leave them with an abstraction of work rather than the ability to work. For my part, I try to make sure my classes create a bridge between seriousness of intent of academic respectability, providing perspectives and facts grounded in rigorous academic research, and useful applicability in real settings, delivering practical tools and real-world examples so that my students may take theory into practice.

Now let's think of the successful professional in today's competitive jobs environment. Twenty-five years ago, you needed to understand what the internet was and what it meant. Ten years ago, you needed to understand the cloud and why it was changing networked systems. Today, you have to assimilate information about technologies like blockchain and artificial intelligence, as well as the business process changes necessitated by the pandemic. In five years, it'll be some other disruption, perhaps quantum or nano or something else. Most of my students have been working professionals who need to keep pace with disruptive, technology-driven change, but who also need to excel at their day jobs while doing so. They aren't taking two years off to pursue knowledge. They are trying to pick up innovative skills and capabilities while still employed and building their careers.

How can you keep working and also keep up?

You need to develop better skills for acquiring new information. You need to acquire it faster, you need to understand it more deeply, and you need to stay on top of what is relevant so you can pick up the next set of skills. Education is no longer a fixed duration event (perhaps four years of undergraduate and two years of graduate studies). In the AI-enabled future, you need to be able to acquire new knowledge every six to twelve months.

Sound impossible? It isn't. But it may require retraining your brain. Computer systems can help, and we will discuss this later in the book. However, in order truly to augment your career, you need to begin by augmenting the human computer, your mind.

I have some good news for you: there are certain cognitive skills that you can develop that will help you in your everyday work and also help you navigate and optimize how you work with artificial intelligence. Preparing your brain can help you prepare for the AI future.

Remaking Your Brain

I will suggest five principles that can help you develop greater cognitive flexibility and ability to acquire knowledge, and once you've mastered part of these there are others you can begin to consider:

1. The importance of practice

2. The benefits of reflection

3. Sustained and gradual change

4. Peer learning

5. Creative exploration

1. The Importance of Practice

I feel good about the value of the knowledge in this book, and I feel that I'm sharing important information with you. It's only going to be relevant to you, however, if you try to apply the lessons. If you simply read the book and stick it on your shelf, while it might provide you fodder for some cocktail-party conversation, it's not going to deliver career transformation or position you for better outcomes as more automation enters the workforce. For that matter, definitionally *innovation* is something new and useful that is put into practice. If it's just new but no one uses it, it's an *invention*. And it is on this dimension of innovation that human beings still hold a clear and sustaining edge over machine systems.

When I teach with my colleagues at MIT, University of Oxford, or Imperial College London, the architecture of the classes is designed to weave together *frameworks* (*scaffolding*, in learning-science terms) that help you construct *mental models* with *examples*, so you begin to understand how the idea looks in a real-world setting, and *activities* where the students try out their own interpretations of the ideas. My frequent collaborator, Professor Alex Pentland, likes to say that the meaningful learning in his classes happens outside the classroom: it's happening in small group discussions among teams of students who are taking the academic frameworks and converting them into something they intend to apply in a tangible setting.

Building a mental model will help convert your practice into longer-term knowledge. Mental models are where you abstract a set of facts or ideas into a framework, which then helps you address a new situation that might not be exactly identical to what you studied. It relates to how your brain is more like a machine learning system than it is an expert system. Peter Senge describes mental models as an internal picture of how the world works.[2]

If you train and practice exhaustively throwing a hard, solid cricket ball a fixed distance in a windless environment like a closed room, you might achieve adequate performance at throwing that one type of ball in that one setting. You won't necessarily have a construct of different types of balls or the effects of wind and gravity on throwing different distances. Faced with an air-filled beach ball, you would perform miserably at trying to get it to hit a target with a light breeze. Varied practice can help you construct mental models of different activities as you put theory into action, versus rote memorization of repetitive activity.

As a human being, you are still better at doing a number of tasks than even a very good AI. An autonomous car might have sensors and LiDAR (measuring distance through use of lasers) and lightning reflexes, but it struggles to distinguish stationary and moving objects at times. Tesla's Autopilot, a precursor to truly autonomous vehicles, had its first human fatality in 2016 when it failed to distinguish between a white tractor-trailer against a bright sky, and when the trailer crossed in front of the car, it drove right underneath it, crushing the windshield into the human operator.[3] Your human brain is able to classify "trucks" as a subset of "moving vehicles to watch out for when driving" as well as "sky" and "road," and notice that if a vehicle is suddenly veering in front of you, you should apply the brakes. Your mental models of driving enable you to deal with a variety of circumstances, even if you've only seen blue tractor-trailers or only white cars prior to an encounter, like in the situation that the Tesla failed to handle in 2016. Since then, Tesla has made several advances, of course—its auto-safety report issued immediately prior to the Covid-19 lockdown, covering the first quarter of 2020, showed one accident per 4.68 million miles driven, making it approximately nine times safer than human drivers.[4] Most AIs don't have the same amount of data as Tesla does, and there are numerous AI applications that are more complicated than driving, so—for now—you have your ability to make mental models working strongly in your favor.

2. The Benefits of Reflection

Your brain can only absorb so much knowledge so quickly. "Wait a minute," you might say to me, "you just told me I need to hurry up and learn something new." This is also true. Don't mistake the exhortation for regular acquisition of new skills with a false claim that you can jam the information into your brain quickly. The reason that intensely studying some facts the night before an exam doesn't create durable knowledge is that your mind is pretty good at getting rid of information it doesn't need to hold on to anymore. Once you've sprayed the facts on to the test paper, the memories quickly degrade.

Professors and nonuniversity training professionals love pushing *block classes* or *block training*. The reason is not because it's the best way to teach you; it's because it's more convenient from a schedule perspective. For that matter, the education industry has taught educational participants to think that training is something that you clear out a few days for, do on a retreat over a weekend or for a set of several days in a row, and that you can "get it out of the way." It runs contrary to how our brains truly function.

What happens when you first encounter new information is that it's kept in short-term memory. Your brain takes in a massive amount of information every day. Most of it is unimportant—do we really need to retain the price of gas that we saw on a sign that we passed while driving on the freeway? We probably remember too many advertisements and internet memes but that's a different discussion. Most of the masses of data that our eyes, ears, and other sense organs process is evaluated in short-term storage, determined not to be salient, and discarded.

Some data, however, is deemed to be worthy of holding on to. Perhaps you have disciplined yourself, as you attempt to learn a new subject, to classify something as important. Maybe you try repeating the fact over and over. By doing so, you are actually strengthening the connections between the neurons that store that data. Your ever-efficient brain will then engage in a process known as *consolidation*, where the chemical and physical structures of the brain move around to shift that particular piece of data from short-term to long-term storage (from the hippocampus to the neocortex, if you want the structural definition).[5]

Sleep is an important part of this process on several levels. It allows for your neurotransmitter reservoirs to replenish, which lets you think more clearly. It lowers your cortisol levels (a stress hormone), which helps you better remember things (high levels of stress have been shown to have a deleterious effect on memory and recall). And one of the major cognitive theories of memory suggests that your brain is performing a form of housekeeping on your memories, moving information around in your brain and putting the important bits into long-term storage.[6]

One tool I like to use when I am forced to teach block classes is to provide an exercise or activity on one day, particularly where the students talk to each other, let the students sleep on it, have them journal and reflect on the prior day's work first thing the next morning, and then discuss the ideas again in an iterative fashion. I find people are able to harvest new insights through this process of engagement, debate, consideration, and revisiting. Professor Marc Ventresca and I used a variation of this technique in a block class we taught at Saïd Business School called Oxford Fintech Lab, which helped propel forward several startups and, according to the students, was a life-changing experience (our last iteration of Oxford Fintech Lab had a net promoter score of 100, which is a measure of client satisfaction—it's impossible to do better than 100).

Your brain does better when it has time to mull over an idea, to reflect on it, and to figure out where that particular piece of information fits within your overall store of knowledge and your array of mental models. It needs to engage in reflection. Ideally, this means you take classes or learn new materials in other ways by spacing out your learning over a period of several weeks.

3. Sustained and Gradual Change

The only way you can build a better way of continuous learning is to engage in sustained change and to allow yourself permission to have it take time. Altering your learning habits is not going to be an instant experience, so you need to be both patient with yourself and disciplined. It's better to set aside thirty minutes every day to work on this instead of trying to do four hours all at once on the weekend. You want to try out new habits a little bit every day, and cumulatively build on those activities.

Think about training for a marathon or even a 10K: you don't wake up one morning, run several hours a day, and five days later run the race. Instead, what you do is start by stretching. You run a few kilometers. You rest for a day. You run a few more kilometers. You rest. Gradually over a period of weeks or months, you prepare your body for the race.

Modifying your learning habits to create an ability to continuously acquire new knowledge is a patient process for which you need to allow time. Learning is intentional. By this I mean you need to set your intention to learn, and very deliberately maintain your discipline of building new memories and new understandings. It's not something that can simply happen to you, and it doesn't come from passively consuming an audiobook or a TED Talk, as intellectually stimulating as those activities can be. They may be part of a path to learning, but they're not sufficient on their own.

For more than fifteen years I had wanted to write books. I had pages of notebooks filled with various scribblings, but the last time I had seriously sat down and written anything of any length was when I took playwriting classes in my undergraduate studies. To migrate from aspirational to actual writer, I began by drafting op-ed pieces and LinkedIn articles about various topics I found interesting (I'm now up to a cumulative 55,000 words on LinkedIn and counting, which is about a full-length business book by itself). I started compiling white papers with coauthors, and eventually edited volumes where I contributed chapters. By the time I sat down to write *Basic Blockchain* (2020), I had a coach lined up to help me crank out the manuscript (we had a very tight deadline), and the comfort of knowing that I could push past creative inertia even if I felt blocked and that I could sit down and write every day. I didn't always write equally well each day, and editing was required, but I was able to crank out the first draft of the manuscript quickly because I had built up the discipline of writing over a two-year period.

Any new discipline, whether it's the discipline of writing, the discipline of learning, or something else altogether, requires both the introduction of new habits and behaviors (which will take some time for you to get used to and begin to engage in fluidly) and the repeated focus to ensure that you stay on your course. Keeping track of your progress, celebrating important milestones, and sharing your achievements with your friends will help you provide yourself with positive reinforcement to keep going.

4. Peer Learning

One of the best ways to learn is through peer education. Medical education, for example, runs on the principle of *watch one, do one, teach one*. It's very high touch, insofar as the ratio of instructor to student is one-to-one or perhaps at worst one-to-four—this is not something that scales. It's lengthy as well: four years of medical school followed by several years of advanced training. However, note that when we want to instill mission-critical learning where lives are literally at stake, we rely on this peer learning-based model.

You'll notice I use words like *learning* a great deal, and I am disdainful of words like *education*. My former business partner Beth Porter and I like to say, "Education is what happens to you, learning is what you do." And instructor-led training is one of the least effective forms of education, the *sage-on-a-stage* model where a learned individual spews forth facts and you are supposed to write them down and figure out what they mean.

The best way I can coach your learning is to provide a little bit of information, then you do something to apply it, ideally in a group, then I provide a little more information, we discuss it as a group, then you go off and work on your own trying to apply the information and elaborate on what I've said. Finally, we come back together as a group and we (not just me, but all of us) critique the various projects to provide further insight.

I have run into impatient students who resist the group-project model. "Why should I have to be stuck with a bunch of people who aren't as smart as I am?" I have been asked this, in one form or another, repeatedly over the years. I have observed that some of the students who protest most vociferously about being allocated to a team are among those who benefit the most from the team activities.

One of the benefits of peer learning is that if you are forced to explain a subject to someone else, you tend to understand it better yourself. Your intuitive grasp of a particular topic, which might be half-organized in your mind, acquires greater structure and solidity when you are required to reduce its principals to an explainable form that someone else can absorb.

Here's some interesting research out of MIT from a few years ago: the scientists took 699 individuals, divided them up into teams of between two and five, and set them to work on complex tasks. The study participants were evaluated on measures such as intelligence quotient (IQ). The most successful problem solvers were not the teams with the highest average IQ, nor were they the teams that had an individual with the highest IQ (the *surround a genius with minions* strategy). Instead, the teams that performed the best, that had the highest *collective intelligence*, were those with an exceptionally high emotional IQ or EQ.[7]

Part of what's going on is the diversity function: having many different perspectives on a problem increases the probability of finding a solution to it. In fact, Northwestern University research conducted on over 3.5 million workers in 154 public companies validates that high levels of diversity, coupled with a disciplined and scaled innovation function, produce the best financial outcomes for corporations.[8]

What is also happening in these dynamic group interactions is that instead of ruminating on the problem inside their own heads, the team dynamic forces individuals to begin to trade concepts back and forth, strengthening the best solutions and discarding the flawed ones.

Over the past decade, Professor Pentland, one of the authors of the original collective intelligence study, worked with Beth Porter and me to create a repeatable way to measure these interactions (known as *instrumenting* them); to begin to stage interventions on them; and over time to optimize team performance, whether that's in a learning setting or other kinds of activities. We created a spinout company around this called Riff Analytics that conducted US National Science

Foundation–funded studies in these areas.[9] As you will learn in chapter 9, we have discovered you can obtain better learning outcomes or craft new knowledge if you bring together the right mix of people in the right kind of structured environment, and have AI help you work better together.

5. Creative Exploration

Mastering peer learning can also open up more possibilities of creative exploration. Creative exploration (or *serious play* as the LEGO corporation would have it) is a building block that leads to other, more advanced concepts such as gamification and complex problem-solving. In the AI future, any analytic or quantitative task is going to be done faster, more accurately, and with greater scalability by a machine. The role of humans will be focused on emotional intelligence-dependent functions where creativity and inventiveness are required. So far we haven't succeeded in creating an artificial intelligence system that is creative by the definition that we use in human systems.

How can we make ourselves better at creative exploration?

Someone might derisively describe an individual as having "the mind of a child." When I hear this expression, I associate it with being open to new experience, neuroplasticity (meaning your brain can readily adapt to new ideas and is better at learning), and being endlessly inventive. The rigid ordering of conventional educational systems takes that creativity and playful spirit and typically shaves off any bits that don't conform to a dogmatic adherence to memorization and regurgitation of fact. We then expect these people to go into the world and build new businesses or solve problems for society. Some of us are lucky: we have exposure to a well-designed undergraduate experience that focuses on critical thinking instead of storing facts. Storing facts becomes increasingly useless as the rate of change of knowledge accelerates. Critical thinking is timeless.

Children engage in creative exploration all the time. They do so solo, making up imaginary friends or scenarios. They do so in groups, collectively envisioning heroic settings or strange new worlds. Listening and talking to each other, they trade ideas back and forth, experimenting with concepts, throwing them away effortlessly, and trying out others as they endlessly create.

A famous creative collaboration experiment known as the marshmallow challenge has been conducted globally with many different types of groups. In eighteen minutes, with limited resources (a marshmallow, some string, tape, and twenty pieces of uncooked spaghetti), competing teams work to build the tallest tower. It opens a fascinating window into problem-solving and group dynamics. Tom Wujec has a wonderful TED Talk explaining the key insights that is worth reviewing.[10]

Here are some of the findings.

Five-year-olds are among the top-performing groups. MBA and law students are among the worst-performing team configurations, as they waste precious minutes navigating status and planning. They are searching for the one best answer, rather than experimenting and discarding several ideas rapidly. Five-year-olds jump in, immediately start trying out different configurations, with subtle social signaling as they grab pieces and interact with one another. What's notable is that not only do the teams of young children perform well, but that it's a team activity, rather than a single designer coming up with the idea. And the children often produce the most interesting structures.

The most vibrant, scalable, and repeatable innovations tend to come from creative collaborations, not solo genius. Diversity, as it turns out, is a necessary input to effective ideation. Social scientists may refer to this as the *law of weak ties*, but the core concept is that many different perspectives being brought to bear on a problem often can reveal unexpected avenues of solutions, or even open up new solution spaces. People who all come from the same backgrounds and cultures tend to bring the same collection of mental models, fact bases, and modes of thought. The more different perspectives you can introduce into a brainstorming discussion, the greater the likelihood you can fabricate creative collisions that produce truly breakthrough thinking.

Accordingly, when you need to solve a complex problem at work, think about who you solve that problem with. Who can you enlist to assist you with the analysis and generation of potential solutions? How can you diversify your creative inputs to the process? Perhaps you can *opinion shop* ideas with a variety of colleagues rather than simply attempting to resolve the issue alone. You could bring several colleagues from different functional areas or cultures together, possibly augmented by external experts, and conduct a focused brainstorming session around the problem.

READING LIST

Out of necessity for brevity we have applied a superficial lens on cognitive flexibility. If you want to dive more deeply into how the mind actually works, Daniel Kahneman's *Thinking, Fast and Slow* (2011) is a good place to start, or if you want a less dense treatise, read Chip and Dan Heath's *Decisive* (2013). Other books like Mark McDaniel, Peter Brown, and Henry Roediger's *Make It Stick* (2014) are specifically focused on learning. Sanjay Sarma and Luke Yoquinto's *Grasp* (2020) makes a valiant effort to summarize and explain an entire body of cognitive and neuroscience research around learning.[11] James Clear's *Atomic Habits* (2018) is a useful guide to shifting your behavior a little bit each day, which can help you develop new learning capabilities. For a bit of fun, Austin Klein's *Steal Like an Artist: 10 Things Nobody Told You about Being Creative* (2012) can help you appreciate the difference between being creative—our goal here—and being original, which is not necessarily needed.

One of the crucial tasks in unleashing your creative exploration capabilities is getting in touch with the imaginative part of your brain, which the educational system has worked to diminish. You can do this through a variety of individual exercises, such as writing or drawing. You can engage in meditation to clear distracting thoughts and mindfulness to gain heightened awareness of yourself and your surroundings. And if you are looking to excel, you will find ways that you can participate in creative play with others.

. . .

Now that we've taken the time to understand what good learning looks like, I'm going to talk about which subjects are best positioned in the AI future. This conversation isn't limited to what subject you ought to study if you are university age, because with the rate of technology evolution increasing, we are entering an era where you will want to acquire new skills every few years, and eventually every year, to remain relevant.

Although education revolution is needed, for now most of the world's employers expect you to show up with a credential from a recognized institution, at the very least an undergraduate degree. Even if you are past school age, as you probably are, you may have children, cousins, nieces, or nephews who are thinking about what to study. My children will be graduating from school into the face of society's AI max Q (what the aeronautical engineers call peak dynamic pressure, or the point in a rocket launch when the body of the rocket is undergoing maximum stress). As a university teacher, what would I tell my own children to study?

Chapter 4: The Rundown

- Untraining and retraining your way of thinking may better prepare you for the AI future.

- Engaging in regular application of the five principles of cognitive flexibility can give you transformational results.

- Creative exploration may be the most powerful of these principles, and it is often best performed as a team versus individual activity.

5

Future Proofing

What to Study and Which Industries Are Safer

Chapter 5: What You Need to Know

- Creative professions and philosophy may be most resistant to AI disruption—and may have unexpected job utility.

- Professions with sustained human contact, like health services, psychotherapy, and hospitality, will be more resistant to AI displacement.

- Emotional intelligence and other *soft skills* represent key job capabilities that AI will have difficulty replicating.

When you think about job security, and what you might want to pursue in undergraduate studies today, you would probably imagine that computer programming would be a good field. After all, if AI is everywhere, don't you want to develop an understanding of the technology that runs our lives? Computer programmers will be replaced first by systems that are *no code*—wherein a human can simply tell the computer what it wants to happen—and eventually by AIs that design themselves. Perhaps the last human programmers to go will be those whose focus is on the theoretical design and architecture behind systems, but there exists the very real possibility that twenty years from now we will be looking at a world where *computer architects* will be fairly abstract conceptualists, or possibly the software engineering function will consist of a single administrator who provides broad guidance to an array of machines. While not an immediate-term worry for next year or the year after, the matter of job security becomes more pressing as we look ahead ten or twenty years and think about career longevity.

The answers to the question, "Which subject areas are best suited to the AI future?" might surprise you.

A Brief Aside on What *Not* to Study

Programming languages, a degree in blockchain, any applied field that is heavy on analytics and computation—these are all likely to be displaced by smart machines or made obsolete by technology innovation. On multiple occasions in recent years I have had to dissuade people from pursuing a PhD in fintech and encourage them to think about foundation-based degrees such as Financial Services or Technology Innovation with a thesis that focuses on fintech but provides them longer-term benefits that go beyond a five- to ten-year tech cycle. Automotive engineering, too, may be a labor of love more than profit: we have very likely passed peak auto ownership, and are seeing the effects of technology-enabled cars, ride-sharing systems, and the rise of autonomous vehicles.[1]

The accounting professions, once considered among the safest career paths, actuarial students and even pre-law, as we reviewed earlier, all are meaningfully at risk. We're setting aside the trades, because this discussion is focused on university education, but it's worth mentioning that everything from welding to window cleaning faces a high likelihood of robotic automation.[2]

Credo Quia Absurdum Est

As I mentioned at the outset of our voyage together, philosophy may provide an intriguing platform from which to enter the field of artificial intelligence. The future AI programmer may be more in dialogue with the machine than giving orders to it and will need a grounding in critical reasoning and formal logic. Conversational AI, and AIs that don't require computer programming in order to get them to do something, are frontier fields that are rapidly maturing into market realities. Indeed, nearly ten years ago Oxford professor and physicist David Deutsch postulated that philosophy could be the key to enabling artificial general intelligence,[3] and his statement holds as much validity today as it did back then.

Philosophy, however, offers a grander field of view than just AI development. As tech billionaire Mark Cuban noted at the South by Southwest festival in 2017, a philosophy degree may be able to help you assess facts and circumstances with a keener eye and take in the bigger picture.[4] He should know—his fortune was created by launching Broadcast.com. Not only did Cuban spot the trend of rich media over the internet, he understood the importance of intellectual property rights to airing professional sports over digital media; he was not only perspicacious enough to identify the gap in the market but skillful enough to execute with his partners on securing those rights. The big picture led to a big payoff, not (directly) a better technology.

Credo quia absurdum est. I believe because it is absurd.

Spark of Creativity

The creative arts remain a uniquely human endeavor. While you may see AIs essaying digital quill and brush to create art, I find the images lack empathy, regardless of how exciting they may be from a conceptual standpoint. There is an indescribable emotional affinity conveyed by a human artist that machines still lack, whether that be in fine arts or in performance.

Design, too, is a field where machine inventions remain a novelty and a bit limited, and at a minimum a human mind directing a machine implementer seems more likely than wholly replacing humans throughout the aesthetic process. Notwithstanding advances in artificial intelligence systems, the human touch is still essential to marrying meat-based cognition (i.e., *Homo sapiens*) with silicon-based technology.

I asked Sanjeev Vohra, who managed tens of thousands of AI developers for Accenture, what advice he would give his own children, or my children, for a stable career when they graduate. Vohra has a son who just finished university and wants to go into a new specialty area at the interface of people and machines. As he puts it, "designing AI to meet the human."

Just as the digital media era brought user experience (UX) design to the fore, the artificial intelligence era is bringing forward this AI interface design role. Vohra's tantalizing hint of an answer lies in the field of bringing human ingenuity to smoothing the interface between human and machine.

The Human Touch

Health care remains a field where in the foreseeable future—ten, twenty, or possibly thirty years—humans are still needed front and center in the experience. Not only doctors, but nurses, pharmacists, physicians' assistants, physical therapists, and other health-care professionals. While AI is beginning to show up in various areas of medicine in a supporting role, such as cancer diagnostics and treatment plan recommendation,[5] it is ultimately human decision-makers who are accountable, and human medical professionals working with the patients. Dentists and dental technicians represent a skilled profession that will be difficult any time in the next twenty to thirty years to replace with AI-powered robots.

It's not only moral and ethical judgment made by humans that accompanies deciding a course of treatment. If a medical professional interacts positively with a patient, they are more likely to follow care instructions and even engage in spontaneous activity to help their health journey. When patients develop an emotional connection with their health professionals centered on trust, it leads to better health outcomes.[6] This is not yet something that can be readily replicated by a machine dispensing care instructions.

The Art of the Mind

Psychology, neuroscience, and cognitive psychology are all fields that benefit from AI tools and enhancements, but there remains a need for human invention, interpretation, and interaction. Notwithstanding our good friend ELIZA, effective therapy requires human-to-human connection. While some organizations are experimenting with creating emotional robot companions, some of which show early promise, we are still years away from fully replacing the functions of a trained therapist, or the nuance and finesse exhibited by an industrial psychologist employed within a large organization. Teaching a computer to understand the intricacies of the human brain to help a patient become more high-functioning and self-actualized is beyond the grasp of today's AI systems, and probably tomorrow's AI systems. The day after tomorrow may see a different kind of AI emerging, which we will address later.

Preparation for the Unknown

Knowledge becomes commodified in a world where we all may have access to brain implants that feed us data in real time. Facts and figures are at everyone's top of mind, on demand. It's the inverse of today's *Google brain* where people have grown forgetful because all knowledge is but a search bar away. Instead, we may have a world of machine enablers tied to our consciousness, constantly feeding us what we need to know, when we need to know it, and in the process accelerating our throughput of information. This is, perhaps, a glimpse of what Accenture's Vohra is talking about when he describes the dawning age of intelligence.

The concept of a tighter linkage between people and how they obtain and use information through machine filters also introduces the risk of greater fragmentation of society and greater bias. If the machine assistants we employ to feed us data apply screens that have been improperly designed or perhaps improperly evolved, we can find ourselves down a very narrow path of thought. If your brain implant discovers you are uncomfortable with certain areas of thought—perhaps you chafe at certain information that disagrees with what you currently believe—will it helpfully try to make your life better by not showing you information it perceives you don't like? This is, in essence, what has already happened with Facebook's algorithms, to deleterious effect as people are polarized into an array of fragmented echo chambers where they only interact with other people who agree with them. It does not take a great imaginative leap to perceive a future where this *Facebook effect* becomes commonplace across all modes of assisted access to knowledge, whether sold by Mr. Zuckerberg or by another technology titan.

Ahead of that more dangerous vision, we continue to see encroachments by AI into more and more professions, coupled to an increasing rate of technology innovation across society. Therefore, the undergraduate education that can prepare one for the AI future may be universally grounded in critical thinking, cognitive flexibility, and studies that foster emotional intelligence. In a world where AIs assume repetitious, analytical tasks, soft skills assume greater importance. This reverses an educational trend of the past thirty or so years favoring preprofessional tracks like finance or business or computer programming, increasingly steering students into semivocational training for perceived *safe* jobs. Engineering schools rose to preeminence, while small liberal arts colleges withered. Now, however, the need may grow for liberal arts education.

Because no one gets a degree in soft skills, what are the courses of study that can help you prepare for an AI future?

There are certain disciplines and associated cocurricular activities that actively develop soft skills. Philosophy, creative writing, and dramatics can all lead to interactions with others that hone both critical thinking and problem-solving in groups. An English language student who is the editor of the university newspaper learns to deal not only with language, but also with motivating and managing teams of people who aren't working for money but instead take pride in the work that is being done. Getting a group of lightly organized undergraduate students to engage, focus, and meet deadlines with, at best, remuneration comprised of pizza and beer requires nothing short of a virtuoso performance in leadership and emotional intelligence.

Emotional Intelligence

The soft skills ingredients for emotional intelligence were for many years dismissed in education in favor of teaching more tangible facts, figures, and capabilities. What's interesting to observe, as awareness of the relationship between soft skills and corporate success rises, is the growing focus of institutions on identifying, hiring for, and cultivating emotional intelligence, or EQ, in their workforce. The field is still in its infancy; managers trained in traditional methods will pay lip service to the need for EQ and then promote for, and incentivize around, quantitative skills (because they are easier to measure)—at least until they make entire departments redundant by replacing them with AI. Emotional intelligence is harder to outsource to a machine, although newer forms of AI include those that actually help measure and develop EQ, as we will discuss in part III.

Before we do, however, it would be beneficial to extend our discussion around areas of study into a strategic lens on defensible industries. Where do you want to develop your career path in a manner that is resilient to potential automation from AI? Which industries will prove to be the most resilient to the AI future, or at a minimum are best positioned to benefit from AI technologies?

With this compound question, I have to admit it is a struggle to argue compelling answers. There is no one industry that is entirely AI proof, no magic sinecure that will provide thirty or forty years of untouched income. Where there are people, there is labor. Where there is labor, there is cost, and with cost, the inexorable forces of capitalism and the public markets will drive toward creating market efficiencies, that is, reducing labor. Some countries, such as Germany, have involved labor unions in the governance of the company, but protecting high-wage jobs will create natural inefficiencies when competing against companies housed elsewhere.

Gerard Verweij, global data & analytics leader for consultancy PwC, said, "No sector or business is in any way immune from the impact of AI."[7] I am inclined to agree. You can run, but you cannot hide. However, you can focus on industries that are more resilient to AI disruption and apply yourself within those industries in a way to extend your lead over the machines. In my work with Evercore ISI, we found that by one measure nearly 100 percent of employment would, in some fashion or another, be touched by AI.

The answers to AI adaptability—career areas that help you evolve along with the evolution of AI—will align with the selection of the best undergraduate studies I described previously, but also include blue-collar professions. The industries most protected require creativity, emotional intelligence, and other soft skills, or they require capabilities for which robots are impractical at our current state of the art.

Health

Health services will remain the province of human practitioners, for the most part, for some time. Select areas of medicine such as radiology or diagnostics are showing suggestive results where AIs equal or outperform human doctors,[8] but current standards of care in medicine require a human decision-maker with human accountability. Additionally, patients prefer interacting with people, particularly in areas like physical care. We have yet to create an AI-powered robot that can give a bed bath that people feel comfortable with. Not because we can't automate robotic medical bathing—more than a decade ago, researchers at Georgia Tech created a robot that demonstrated it could give sponge baths[9]—but rather because most people would rather receive empathy and care from another human being.

In the more distant future, when truly humanoid robots emerge that are indistinguishable from people, or if a generation raised on Roombas reaches retirement age and is fine with being touched by machines for intimate personal care, this may change, but until then the human health worker is secure.

Live Performing Arts

Live performances, whether theater, music, or dance, remain a domain that benefits from the human touch. Human beings are tribal and pack-like, and have an intrinsic need for connection with each other that can be modulated through live performance.[10] Watching a prerecorded performance isn't the same; it loses the feedback loop that a performer creates with an audience.[11] Until we can create humanlike robots that very closely resemble human performers and are able to interact with an audience dynamically to create a connection with the audience, we will need human performers. The electric connection that is created by a crowd that is going through a shared experience is difficult to replicate in a digital environment. For prerecorded music, AI-generated product has started appearing—but not yet at a quality where it would create a chart-topping hit. Legal issues have begun proliferating as well around a host of copyright-related matters.[12]

Retail, Hospitality, and Other Personal Services

I recall when the e-commerce boom was first gaining momentum in the 1990s that people were worried Amazon and eBay would spell the end of in-person retail. To a degree, this prognostication was correct: Amazon is exploring converting abandoned JC Penney and Sears stores into warehouse facilities inside shopping malls.[13] At the same time, people still prefer to see, touch, and try on items where they can. Even mighty Amazon has been exploring a high-tech variant of real-world shopping, albeit with a high-tech twist: there's no checkout, you simply walk out of the store and wireless transmitters on your phone and on the products you are buying take care of your purchase automatically.[14] And, of course, they made a $13.7 billion bet on acquiring gourmet grocery Whole Foods.[15] Restaurants, likewise, are not a robot-friendly environment. People prefer human servers in most countries.

Other personal services remain stubbornly personal, and likely will for some time. Massage therapy and physical therapy remain hands-on, personally delivered services, in spite of various massage chairs and other machines that can move and stretch the body. Hair stylists and nail technicians are likely to be difficult to replace by machines, as much for the personal interaction in the salon as for the technical intricacies of the work. It's hard to feel pampered by a robot.

We may, however, end up seeing a class-based bifurcation. As robot labor gets cheaper and cheaper, we may see lower-end delivery by machines with the human touch reserved for the posh experience. It's difficult to argue that the McDonald's restaurant worker adds significant value over a machine. You could more quickly and more cheaply get your gut-busting fast food from a robotic system, and you wouldn't need a very smart AI to run it. Conversely, it is easy to imagine that twenty years from now you will still talk to the (human) maître d' at Chiltern Firehouse in London or Waku Ghin in Singapore or take a recommendation from the sommelier at Le Bernardin in New York.

Energy Systems

Installing wind farms or solar panels will still require people in the next ten or twenty years. Further out, it may be possible for robotic labor to replace humans; for now, we are still reliant on human hands to erect wind towers or place panels. The power industry, more broadly, relies on human implementation and deployment of power systems, and at least some human intervention on the maintenance of them. Partly, there are mechanisms that still benefit from the human touch. Partly, there is the conscious decision not to put an AI completely in control of, say, a nuclear power plant, but instead to require human-in-the-loop technology. Extractives such as oil and coal, despite various bits of automation, still rely on a significant amount of human labor, both upstream and downstream.

Construction

Although I am not as sanguine as some with respect to the ability of the construction industry to resist automation, there is an argument that says it will be a very long time before AI displaces human. This is to some extent due to the nature of the work, given that the ground-level hand labor in home construction occurs in a wide variety of uncontrolled environments with numerous variables, which a moderately trained twenty-five-year-old human can easily handle but a very expensive and sophisticated robot today struggles with. To some extent, it is because of the industry structure of construction, with numerous specialized subcontractors working under the direction of a general contractor. Each element of home building has an array of complex choices and these different choices—ranging from what kind of fixtures you choose to the kind of flooring you put in—need to seamlessly integrate with one another.[16] While in theory robots can do parts of these tasks, and in theory you can assemble prefabricated homes with the design selected from a catalog and the parts snapped together out of a kit, most people don't. New home construction is the purview of builders operating in a complex ecosystem of contractors.

Government

The industry of government will be among the last to accept widespread adoption of AI systems. I don't mean selective use of AI for certain purposes—the company Palantir has reached nearly $1 billion of revenue from a handful of government contracts—but rather widespread replacement of human government workers with AI systems. I refer specifically to the staff professionals in government versus politicians. While Japan may have had an AI mayoral candidate,[17] that is an outlier event rather than an immediate trend. The rank-and-file government workers who manage various government departments and programs are likely to remain in place for years to come.

Agriculture and Animal Husbandry

AI is slowly trying to work its way into the agricultural industries, but human labor will be required for the care, feeding, and harvesting of plants and animals. Even with innovations such as vertical farming and farm automation systems, we still have people involved at numerous steps in the farming process. We will need much more powerful and simultaneously less expensive robotic systems (which are perhaps thirty to fifty years away) in order to have widescale replacement of people with machines, particularly in developing countries.

Checklist to Adapt Your Future

The industries that will likely prove best suited for a significant proportion of human involvement, not unlike the individual professions described in chapter 6, rely on one or more of the following characteristics. When you think about career and industry strategy, see how many of these attributes you can attach to a particular area:

- Requires a high degree of empathy or emotional intelligence

- Involves repeated physical contact with human beings, living animals, or plants

- Entails a high degree of judgment in the face of rapidly changing, variable, or novel circumstances

- Benefits from a significant level of creativity or artistic expression

- Persists in requiring intuition for competitive advantage or greater success

And Yet . . .

Thinking of an industry sector that will forever be completely untouched by AI automation is difficult in the extreme. As artificial intelligence gets more sophisticated, the range and nature of fields in which they can be deployed are increasing.

Hiding out in a particular field isn't the answer. If you want to win at work in the age of AI, you need to find ways to make AI work *for* you, rather than *against* you, augmenting your capabilities, rather than seeking to replicate them.

You will need AI and digital literacy to succeed, even in primarily human-centric professions like design or health services.

The next section will explain what this emerging model of Human+AI hybrids looks like, and how you can bring artificial intelligence into your competitive tool kit.

Chapter 5: The Rundown

- Analytical and quantitative professions are under greatest threat from AI displacement.

- Careers that require human-to-human contact, such as retail, as well as careers that involve complex physical tasks, like energy systems and construction, will take longer to disrupt than other domains.

- Ultimately, most professions will face some degree of AI disruption over time. The key to success will be learning how to work in collaboration with AI versus in competition with it.

6

What Can Human+AI Systems Do?

Adventures in Collective Intelligence and More

Chapter 6: What You Need to Know

- Human+AI systems can help improve how people collaborate in teams.

- Outcomes in critical domains, such as health services, can be improved through engaging artificial intelligence alongside human experts.

- AI digital agents (imagine your own version of *Iron Man*'s JARVIS) may represent the most powerful application of Human+AI technology.

- Human+AI hybrid systems can even predict the future.

Envision the everyday, run-of-the-mill business or project meeting. The average manager spends 35 to 50 percent of their time in meetings. It's a setting ripe for enhancement by artificial intelligence.

A group of people gather together in a room or on a video-conference call. If they're lucky, the meeting has an agenda attached to it. If they're really lucky, someone is facilitating the meeting and the agenda is even followed. This group has a conversation or discussion. Perhaps it's a brainstorming session, where several new ideas are generated, evaluated, and either agreed on or discarded. Perhaps it's a decision meeting where facts are presented and members select from several choices to determine a course of action.

Whatever the meeting type, there's a form of conversation. If good practices are being employed, not only is there an agenda, but also a meeting scribe who records what was said and generates the meeting minutes. Unfortunately, most meetings aren't structured using best practice, which undoubtedly contributes to the estimation that executives believe that 67 percent of meetings are failures, wasting over $37 billion each year in unproductive yakking.[1]

Even productive meetings that have positive, desired outcomes are suboptimal compared to what they could be. I recently helped a group of half-a-dozen senior executives who were developing innovation and growth projects centered on novel uses of data. I was facilitating a brainstorming meeting to generate twenty new business ideas in forty minutes (a body of literature has been written about the benefits of design-constrained innovation). After providing some context on the span of time and scope of opportunity, and the types or modes of innovation we wanted to use, I put a blank slide on to the screen and we began populating the page with business ideas.

I had to listen carefully to each person speaking. The video-conferencing software didn't help much with the crosstalk, but at least I could see people to call on them when their body language indicated a desire to contribute something. My attention was split across multiple tasks. I needed to monitor everyone in the meeting, making sure they were all contributing. I needed to interpret what they were saying *and* capture it in the appropriate place. I needed to unpack their ideas, as some of the suggestions were in fact divisible into two or three distinct venture concepts. One hundred percent of my focus was on facilitation. It meant I didn't do much to contribute my own ideas (I think I came up with one in this particular conversation), but that wasn't my role in the meeting. It *couldn't* be my role in the meeting, because my mental processing was focused on the soft and hard aspects of meeting facilitation. In forty minutes we generated twenty ideas, and then laid out a timeline with accountability attached. I found myself wishing I had been able to spend more time thinking and elaborating on the discussion, and not have had to interpret and record it.

A friend and former business partner of mine, Tom Gardner, developed some interesting meeting management techniques in his years of leadership. Tom was chairman of pharma software company Integrichain, is the former CEO of what was a billion-dollar public company, Datamonitor, and before that rose to fame as the marketing executive at Johnson & Johnson who took over-the-counter Tylenol. He's now enjoying a flourishing career as an angel investor and civic booster in Sarasota, Florida, part of the burgeoning tech scene that has arisen outside of traditional clusters like Silicon Valley. When I left my position as Ernst & Young's first, and at the time only, entrepreneur-in-residence to form a search fund with Tom, he put me up in his house in Sarasota at the turn of the year, and we mapped out the future. (The successful search generated enough fees for me to switch tracks for a while and get a job at MIT, which is a story for another book.)

A big, bluff man with ruddy cheeks and an imposing disposition, Tom played professional football (American-style) briefly before going into business. Relentlessly fascinated with innovation, Tom was an early adopter of tablets, and would regularly carry his with him to meetings. As we would sit and talk, he would industriously type away at the tablet, taking notes on our discussion as we'd go. It was, candidly, a little distracting; at the same time, at the end of every meeting he would instantly generate an email for the both of us (and whoever we were meeting with), describing what we said, what we decided, and our next steps with assigned responsibilities.

Good discipline, for certain. It's one of those management hacks that captures relevant knowledge while it's fresh in the mind and sets up future accountabilities. You start to get a window into how Tom effectively ran a billion-dollar public company.

Yet at the same time, here we were consuming the mental cycles of a brilliant business leader tapping away at his keyboard. He wasn't focused on me, on my body language; he wasn't making eye contact. His oversized fingers, well-suited for gripping a pigskin or for crushing your hand in an overwhelmingly dominant handshake, instead were pecking away at a little electronic device, taking down our conversation. Tom's attention focused on his screen, and not on the people in the room with him, which resulted in a diminution of social signaling within the dyad or group. Eighty percent of the social signals we respond to in collaborations come from body language. All of that is lost if someone is typing and not watching.

It turns out that the social cues we exchange when we sit near one another and interact are significantly more beneficial than some people might suspect. It turns out that they are essential for the creation of trust among parties. On a preverbal, typically subconscious level, we are engaged in a variety of signaling behaviors when we interact with each other in person. If I cross my arms, you might cross your arms in a form of mimicry. If you feel connected to what I am saying, you might open up your body stance, and perhaps encourage me to continue to speak with a nod, with a gesture of your hand or with a nonlinguistic audio cue ("uh-huh," "hmm," etc.).

All of those signals of personal connectivity and emotional linkage are lost if you are focused on your device instead of on my face.

Meetings, Reimagined

What if there were a different version of reality?

Computer systems have required sophisticated programming in order to learn how to address and manipulate unstructured data like human speech. Siri, Google Voice, Amazon Echo—these are technologies that can extract words or even sentences out of spoken language. They're pretty good at English, as they started out being trained by engineers in the western United States (and other tech clusters) in English language. For many of my books, increasingly, I am able to dictate a third to half of my content, and the built-in transcription in the iPhone is able to understand me reasonably well. My editor can share with you how much my words still need to be corrected, but it's a huge leap forward from the speech-to-text systems of the 1990s that you used to have to *train* by reading prerecorded scripts to them. In 2023, a straight-out-of-the-box consumer electronic can understand almost anyone (typically speaking in English) and provide 95 percent or better accuracy even under less-than-ideal conditions. The other 5 percent is the subject of numerous jokes in popular culture.

Me: "Alexa, play 'Despacito.'"
Alexa: "Praying for desperados."

These current-generation AI systems are less proficient when confronted with the thirty-eight languages used by Bangladesh's 161 million citizens, as I discovered when I met with the country's Minister of Telecommunications to talk about his interests in better artificial intelligence as a means of promoting access and inclusion in his society. Large segments of the population are illiterate as well, so a conversational system (not based on English-language AI) was needed that could understand and respond in thirty-eight languages and multiple dialects. Off-the-shelf AI wouldn't work for them. They needed a smarter artificial intelligence. What they wanted was even more ambitious: Could this AI actually understand what people meant and make recommendations to them when they called up the government for help with their taxes, finding a job, getting food aid, or dealing with a housing issue?

Meeting of Minds

Let's revisit that supposedly well-constructed meeting we talked about earlier, and pretend we had artificial intelligence engaged in idea learning. Imagine if a conversational AI were listening in on the discussion between Tom Gardner and me, automatically generating notes of what we said using speech-to-data. Imagine further that the AI was tied into our calendars and emails, so it had some ideas around the context of our conversation. Imagine that AI was able not only to transcribe our words, but also understood the meaning behind them, and was able to extract the major themes of our discussion, pick up the verbal cues of people being assigned responsibilities, and sketch out a project plan.

In this new kind of human–machine hybrid interaction, we could look each other in the eye and focus on each other, with an AI in the background acting as an enabling digital assistant. The AI could even populate follow-up meetings into our calendars. The drudgery of transcription, note-taking, and scheduling would get lifted from our shoulders so we could focus on higher-order thinking.

A piece of software known as Otter.AI can take care of this for us today. With a few tweaks, it could tie into our project management software, assign and track tasks, and help us stay on plan.

Imagine what an organization could look like if AI minders were keeping track for us of what we want to remember. Imagine the improvements in efficiency if we didn't have follow-up items slip through the cracks, if we had an unobtrusively helpful machine reminding us of key workflow priorities, helping us manage our teams and ourselves better so that a project could come in ahead of schedule and under budget. Further, imagine if these AI systems could assess probabilities around delivery, and could help us adjust if problems were forecast to arise.

Healthy Machines

The Human+AI revolution is not limited to the meeting room or the boardroom. Imagine what these smart AI assistants could do in a hospital setting. This new generation of AI assistants could actually help save lives.

One of the major causes of death in hospitals is attributable to something known as "transitions in care." It's a term to describe what happens when a patient is transferred from one medical provider to another. Over 3 million people die every year, according to the World Health Organization, due to medical error. Poor communications among medical professionals is one of the top factors leading to these deaths.

Let's imagine that you are in your home and suddenly experience respiratory distress. Your friend, spouse, or partner calls an ambulance. The emergency medical personnel in the ambulance are the first care providers to interact with you. They take vital signs, check your breathing, listen to your pulse. They're capturing this information in some form, but maybe they don't have time to write it down accurately because they are busy saving your life.

The ambulance pulls up to the hospital. Rushing you off on a gurney, the medical technician quickly runs through your symptoms with the nurse or doctor at the emergency department. Did they remember everything accurately? Did they transmit all of the vital information?

The emergency physicians work on you but it doesn't seem to be solving your respiratory distress. Your anxiety goes through the roof as the beeping of the machines and the moans of the other patients add to an already stressful situation. You spiral further. Your throat closes over, and they aren't able to put a tube down your throat to help you breathe. The emergency physicians have to perform a tracheotomy, a procedure where they cut open part of your throat to directly access your windpipe and help you breathe. You are stabilized, for now, but you are in bad shape. They transfer you to the intensive care unit (ICU). A nurse brings a wheeled stretcher to carry you from the emergency department up to the ICU. The nurse then explains your symptoms and reviews your chart with the new physician looking after you in the ICU.

At each patient handoff from one care provider to the next—from ambulance technician to emergency department physician to nurse to ICU physician—there is a conveyance of information. Was all the information transmitted correctly? Was enough of it captured in your chart—the set of documents that describes you, your medical history, your condition, how you were treated, and what drugs were administered?

Electronic medical records (EMR) were supposed to help address these issues, but as one doctor described it to me, she's now staring at a machine instead of keeping her eyes on the patient. Many of the critical cues about patient health that are picked up from visual observation are now absent because she's making sure that the EMR system is accepting the data. One of the more enlightening TEDMED Talks that I have heard proposed a revolution in medicine, a world in which we'd have not only doctors without borders, but also doctors without keyboards. It's no wonder when you understand the strategy behind EMR software companies. The chief medical officer of one of the three largest explained to me that the customer they serve isn't the doctor or nurse. It's the CFO of the hospital. EMR systems are optimized to generate financial reports for CFOs, not outcomes for patients. Much becomes clear.

Journey now with me to a world where innovative computer scientists are permitted to integrate their AIs in the hospital setting. The ambulance, the emergency department, even the gurney could be wired up with microphones feeding data to sophisticated artificial intelligences that improve care and even help prevent disease.

AI can do more than listen. Anmol Madan, a frequent buffet-line companion of mine at the World Economic Forum annual meeting in Davos, has started a company called Ginger.io that provides proactive care through AI. Madan began Ginger.io to capitalize on a computational social science breakthrough emerging out of wearable computing developed in Professor Pentland's lab at MIT. Wearables are essentially tiny computers that people take with them everywhere, enabling health measurement to go from a periodic event (you go to the hospital, the doctor evaluates you, you leave) to a continuous event (your Fitbit or a similar device that constantly monitors various signals from your body). Mobile phones are the most ubiquitous wearable in the world, carried with us everywhere we go and packed with sensors. Those sensors generate streams of data, and particularly tuned machine learning systems can extract predictive patterns from that data.

What Madan and his colleagues realized, based on this data, was that people who suffered from chronic mental health conditions such as depression began exhibiting signs of depression before even they were consciously aware of them. They contacted fewer people; they were less social. They went out of their home less, or not at all. They moved around less when they were inside their homes. Sleep patterns were disrupted. They slept too much, too little, or with too many interruptions.

With permission of the user, simple signals from the mobile phone could pick up these disturbances in someone's routine. The individual's medical provider could be contacted to enable an early intervention, before the person has to be hospitalized or worse. Not only was Ginger.io's AI assistant understanding signals about a patient's health, it was also predicting which signals were indicative of serious issues, and facilitating interaction with a health provider through remote delivery in order to address them quickly. We now have continuous protection around our mental health, providing better care, faster, at a lower cost than before.

The privacy implications of these super smart AIs are, of course, profound. There are laws in various countries that govern personal privacy, that dictate how medical information is handled and secured, and the conditions under which it may be shared. All of those rules would need to be taken into account in the AI systems we would deploy into these settings. The European Union and other domiciles have not only instituted strong privacy protections but are putting in place rules and systems around use of artificial intelligence, including with respect to private data.

Activating Human+AI

We've established that we could take a good deal of the tedious, menial work in a meeting and offload it to a machine, and that machine can help keep us, our team, and our project on course around a set of deliverables. We've explored the use of AI helpers in medical settings, whether it's at the hospital or in the home. We could even use AI to reduce the rate of industrial accidents. We are, however, still in the realm of relatively passive systems. The AI assistant who is transcribing our meeting and assigning follow-up tasks is quietly operating in the background. It's unobtrusive. It might extract meaning from the meeting, but it's not directly contributing to the functioning of the team or the quality of the conversation.

To truly bring together the fusion of human and artificial intelligence systems, we need to take the relationship a step further. Beyond listening and understanding, beyond interpreting and forecasting, beyond even connecting, we need to bring the AI into a tighter collaboration with human systems.

We need to have AI power up our teams, as we will discuss shortly. But first, let's go into greater depth around the AI tools that can enable human 2.0.

AI Tools for Human 2.0

AI tools are already beginning to wile their way into your everyday life. However, not all AI is designed to change your political opinion or get you to purchase a new consumer product. It is possible, in fact, to master these technologies and use them to augment your career rather than have AI prey upon you. The first step is to have a heightened awareness of what you do at work and how you interact with technology—this will be the foundation for seeking out new, more powerful AI tools that help you compete and win.

I am not going to dwell on industrial automation systems that operate *in the background*. Yes, we have AI involved in managing public transportation. Yes, auto manufacturing systems have relied on robots for decades. Yes, computers largely are responsible for flying most commercial aircraft, with humans present more as a fail-safe than as primary operators of the equipment. We will set those to one side. Instead, we will look at more personal applications of AI.

We will first look at the omnipresent AI that we might barely notice today, that already helps us out in myriad ways, and expand from there into some newer frontiers of augmentation of human cognition. This hybrid of human and machine systems is something we will call *human 2.0*. It inevitably leads to the question of human 3.0, human 4.0, and so on, which I will address a bit later on in the book.

Invisible Assistants

If you use either Google/Android or Apple (which is close to 100 percent of people with smartphones), you already are encountering invisible AI assistants. These digital minions are scurrying about in the background, touching up our lives here and there, either totally imperceptible or so subtle that we barely notice. For example, as I typed the last sentence, I mis-keyed the letter "n" and accidentally hit the letter "m." Almost faster than I could perceive, my Macbook automatically changed the letter for me.

In general, I find the autocorrect to be pretty accurate, and a jumping off point for other unobtrusive means of AI helping people function better and faster. Google extended the concept further, from analysis of what you have written into predicting what it thinks you are probably going to write: predictive text. With more than 2 trillion searches made annually, and growing, there is a large dataset of the words people most commonly string together for Google to work with.

Google hosts Gmail and began feeding data from its 1.8 billion email users into its language systems.[2] Now, when you open up Gmail and begin typing, it offers you autocompletion options so that you simply hit the right-arrow button to finish the sentence. Called *Smart Compose*, it can dramatically speed up your rate of creating email content by making intelligent guesses as to what you intend to write next and offering you grayed-out text that you can accept by pressing a button.

It usually works pretty well; although for fun I opened up an email and plugged in *"It seems to be struggling a bit to figure out where I am taking this seriously"* instead of "taking this sentence." Unfair test? Perhaps. In my personal experience, however, it gets it right more often than not and can maybe improve my composition speed by about 10 percent.

Yet I'm not entirely certain that helping me generate more message volume is desirable. In the first three weeks of the month in which I wrote this chapter, I determined that I had written over 130,000 words, but only 10,000 were for my book manuscript. I have since adjusted the ratio, but more doesn't necessarily mean better. Emails and text messages are a great way for another person to put something on your "to-do" list, and every missive I send tends to generate a response. Google and others then added various kinds of AI smart-filtering on messages, which works with varying degrees of success (I tend to find important messages get filtered out into spam, and then I need to go hunting for them). Setting aside a socio-cultural or anthropologic examination of my own work habits, these AI tools are both problem and solution to the issues of messaging volume.

Bard is Google's latest entrant into the world of AI, a generative AI system that's also tied to search and other Google tools. Unlike ChatGPT, which at present is only trained on data through 2021, Google Bard is up to date. It also attempts to fact-check itself to stave off hallucinations. Google itself warns that because the system uses real-world text as a source, it is still subject to providing misinformation or displaying bias.[3]

Google is not alone in this quest to bring AI alongside human activity and nudge productivity increases into our workflow and into our lives. Apple assessed billions of encounters between users and their smartphones, and noticed the simple pattern that many people check the weather when they wake up in the morning. Now, when I first wake up and look at my iPhone, it offers me a smart prompt on the lock screen to check the weather without having to unlock the phone or hunt through icons to find the weather app. These little conveniences offer what product marketers call *surprise and delight* in the consumer: I didn't know I wanted that thing, but now that I have it, I like it.

Apple's family of AI assistants is getting better, but still needs a bit of work. They are a dramatic improvement over the transcribers of the past and have transcended the usability threshold. I find anecdotally that iPhone voice transcription works better than 98 percent of the time, although it struggles a bit with my pronunciation of certain words. When I have dictated parts of books, my editor has had to wrestle at times with Apple's creative interpretation of what I actually said: "Flown from it-will, cannot the heavy, there-at, through-at, slopeless and ripe . . ."

To be completely honest, that's a quote from Richard K. Morgan's *Thirteen* (2007), otherwise known as *Black Man*, imagining what machines would create if they were allowed to be creative, but it's in the same family as what Apple's speech-to-text translator sometimes does to my composition. At least a close cousin. If you dig a little more deeply, researchers believe that Apple's system performs less well than those of Google, Microsoft, IBM, and Amazon because it is undertaking on-the-fly transcription rather than waiting for the entire audio snippet before trying to figure out what was meant.[4] Comically, Apple will often get it right for me initially, then reconsider when it gets the whole clip and change sections into aphasic word salad.

I mock these machine systems at my own peril. Every year, they increase their capabilities by one or more orders of magnitude, while in a good year I might improve 1 percent to 5 percent. By some measures, statistically speaking I probably began experiencing a decrease in cognitive performance in my twenties. By other measures, I can look forward to performance decline within the next three years.[5] Conversely, the machines are only getting better, and soon they will be able to take my creative inspiration and turn it into full-fledged articles and books.

AI assistants can make your brain a bit weak, like an underutilized muscle, giving rise to the term *Google brain* for how people no longer retain facts and figures because they are but a few keystrokes away in the search bar. What if, on the other hand, we had AI that could learn what we know, and what we would like to know, and that AI started making suggestions to us throughout our workdays to extend our thinking, perhaps even in new and unexpected directions, but in all instances aligned with our desires and goals?

Let's see what happens if we provide the AI with a bit of a prompt and encourage it to help write this book . . .

Artificial Intelligence Authors

AI writing machines, software systems that can completely replace human authors in all circumstances, remain slightly out of reach. Conversely, some combination of a human starting point and a machine extension, or a machine-generated text that is then edited by humans, is already here. This suggests the tantalizing possibility that the predictive text we already have available to us could be extrapolated at a scale not just of a few words, or the end of a sentence, but to a full-length treatise, all while preserving tone of voice, dialect, and writing style.

I still write my books the old-fashioned way, by hand (well, keyboard). Sometimes I will dictate chapters into my iPhone and clean up the transcript, but it's still me composing. Many colleagues, however, have begun using GPT-4 to write a book in a week! A day! An hour! The quality, I leave as an exercise for the reader. A colleague of mine bragged about writing a new book in five days using generative AI. "Is it any good?" I asked him. "Does it matter?" he replied. Not for me; but some appear to be embracing this approach.

And yet—I am sure publishers are dreaming of the day they can use AI instead of unreliable human authors—business publishers don't even need to dream; they replaced human writers for structured articles like corporate earnings releases around a decade ago.[6]

Second Verse, *Not* Same as the First

I started talking seriously to people about OpenAI and GPT in 2020. The people who see beyond the edge of the map, so to speak, were already contemplating what possibilities would emerge out of conversational AI, and democratizing access to AI systems. I confess that, as excited as I was, as much as I believed it could be transformative, I failed to predict the *speed* with which it would gain adoption once it became accessible to the average person.

AI will also change the very way writers choose to write. In the same way that AI can be used to help a human writer, AI can also be used to help a human decide how to tell a story. This is done by using a process called *natural language generation* (NLG). Three years ago, I predicted that NLG would be able to generate a full text, and that text would be indistinguishable from human-written prose—and here we are.

The breathlessly excited articles that have been written about GPT-4 perhaps even understate its potential impact.

Futurist Arram Sabeti asks what if we begin cocreating our entertainment with an AI? What if our next Netflix binge consisted of us telling the Netflix AI that we wanted a sci-fi space western with 30 percent thriller/intrigue and 10 percent romance? What if the AI generated the six-episode show right on the spot, as we watched, and at critical plot points would ask us for decisions as to what direction the plot should take and then dynamically generate the output? Legions of disappointed *Game of Thrones* fans, myself included, would gladly re-create the final two seasons to provide for a more satisfying denouement, which this technology could enable. The *Black Mirror* episode "Bandersnatch" is but a primitive echo of this future-forward idea of Human+AI entertainment. The 2023 actors and writers strikes in Hollywood acutely reflect the (correct) level of anxiety about what happens if digital systems can create entertainment product with little or no help from humans.

Virtual Assistants

It appears inevitable that we would take the chatbot and merge it with the calendar and other capabilities to create virtual assistants. While this might represent labor displacement for the human admin, it can help the busy entrepreneur or executive be more productive. Some AI assistants have become pretty good. You simply copy them into emails, and queue them to schedule a meeting. The virtual assistant scans through your diary and generates an email to whoever you are meeting, suggesting a few times. It will parse their reply (accepting, declining, or modifying) and then either book the meeting or work with the other parties to find a time that everyone can make happen.

They aren't artificial general intelligence (AGI), but they do add a convenience to your work at a fraction of the cost of hiring a human assistant: digital agent companies charge anywhere between $0 and perhaps $20 a month, depending on how sophisticated a tool you want to use. Compare this to £21,287 per year for an office assistant in London or $49,418 per year in New York City, and you understand why digital assistants have taken off.[7]

When I ask Sanjeev Vohra about how Accenture governs its array of AIs, he lets slip some intriguing tidbits. He might have a business unit, such as business process outsourcing (BPO), which is 30 to 40 percent machines. Those machines include a variety of specialists and contain a command center with thousands of bots running at any time. Poorly functioning bots can be diagnosed, taken to a *sick bay*, treated, and redeployed. A *broken* or *damaged* bot might be one that is doing something erratic, or that veers off in the wrong direction and needs to be realigned. For example, let's pretend we had an automated scheduling bot running people's diaries: imagine if it started putting all meetings at 4 a.m. because it got confused about time zones. There are even some AIs that are self-healing, which is itself a big area of research, but many still need people to help manage them.

Displacement of conventional human assistants? Absolutely. Or at least freeing them up to work on more complex tasks. It has another productivity benefit as well: people who couldn't afford a regular assistant, or who didn't need a full-time one, now can get the efficiency that having someone else run your calendar delivers without anywhere near the associated expense. Overall productivity in the workforce increases, and you as a professional can focus more of your energy on high-value work and less of it on the mundane task of scheduling.

Emotional Intelligence Assistance

Cogito Corporation is a Boston-based spinout from Pentland's lab, focused primarily on one-on-one interactions, particularly over the phone. If you can't see someone face to face, even over video call, you lose a great deal of insight into their emotional reactions to your conversation. In a sales discussion, that can be fatal.

Is it possible to derive emotional signals just from a voice? It turns out you can, very well. By examining how two people interact with each other in a phone call, Cogito can determine if the sales prospect isn't really following along with the agent, and if the agent should slow down, speed up, or jump to another section in their call script.

Very good telephone agents are able to do this instinctively, because they can detect minute variations in someone's voice and pattern of speech. However, it's hard to teach that to large numbers of people, and it's difficult to be consistent; if the human agent is tired or distracted, they'll miss out on those subtle audio cues. AI can step into this gap and help bridge the two ends of the conversation by signaling to the call-center agent what they need to do in order to build a better rapport with the prospect and close the sale.

Cogito has been able to deliver for insurance company Humana a 28 percent improvement in customer satisfaction, and a 63 percent improvement in employee engagement, by taking the capabilities of the average call-center operator and shadowing and nudging them into higher performance.[8] These centaur call-center sales professionals, consisting of a hybrid of a person and AI, are superior to the average human agents.

How do we take this idea of AI-people hybrids beyond one-on-one interactions and into the team setting?

Meeting Mediators

At MIT, Alex Pentland's Human Dynamics group spent years exploring what it takes to make a team, and an organization, function better. After pioneering wearable computing—which proved a rich source of information about people and what they do, particularly when around each other—they turned their attention to questions of how to not only understand but actively influence group interactions for better outcomes. This led them, for example, to figuring out that by changing seating charts in a bank, they were able to dramatically increase productivity by ensuring the right people were talking to each other every day.[9] Research that emerged out of work originally conducted by MIT Human Dynamics determined that happy, productive teams actually send *fewer* emails.[10] Much of this work was conducted with the assistance of little devices called *sociometric badges* that people would wear around their necks like corporate name badges. These devices could figure out who was standing near who (which helped to decipher innovation patterns, because if you stand near someone in an office for fifteen minutes you are probably talking to them; we don't even need to have audio on you to infer this pretty accurately) and a few other neat tricks. All of this, of course, was conducted with the consent of the people involved.

Among other insights, this research led to Pentland's seminal article "The New Science of Building Great Teams," which revealed that you could actually predict which teams would outperform and which teams would underperform simply by observing their patterns of communications in meetings. Furthermore, if you played back to people how they were behaving, the simple act of the positive feedback loop would shift behavior (people would adjust themselves) and you could optimize team performance.[11]

I joined Alex Pentland informally in 2013 and more formally in 2014, as part of my inquisitive quest for innovation hot spots within MIT. One of the first projects I helped with focused on the question of how to scale up the sensing function of the sociometric badges. As much as you can educate people about them, badges felt a little invasive when we used them in real-world environments, such as a major aerospace company. People found them "creepy."

What if we could make the intervention less intrusive? What if we could instrumentalize the videoconference call? Inspired by the idea that the teams that collaborated most effectively spoke and even moved together in a common manner, we called it the Rhythm Project. The metaphor that came up often was that a successful brainstorming or a high-performing team would reveal communication patterns that resembled a group of improvisational jazz musicians.

We took the in-person meeting tool, and we played it out in a digital (virtual) environment. We were really interested to explore this in the forum of online education because we felt that this was a major failure point of massively open online classes (MOOCs), the most popular kind of online learning. Whereas on campus we were able to put students into table exercises and small groups for projects, online the collaboration environments ranged from horrible to really bad. The Rhythm Project worked to develop tools that would help small teams collaborate better in a distance environment.[12]

Work derived from the Rhythm Project was then applied by the government of Canada to the issue of innovating in the field of AI itself. Canada had an issue: it is a major center of AI research, and yet has not seen the same wealth of unicorn-like tech companies like Silicon Valley, New York, or even London. How can it improve the pace of AI commercialization? At the same time, how can a relatively small population, spread over a relatively large geography, enjoy the benefits of this opportunity instead of simply concentrating in Toronto (where the Vector Institute, a major research center, is based).

We created an online accelerator program to help innovators and entrepreneurs apply the technology of AI to new businesses. We used the Pentland AI feedback systems to improve the performance of teams going through the accelerator. Participants in our program were *50 percent* more likely to launch a startup or a new AI initiative in a large company than people going through a very good in-person, on-campus accelerator at MIT. And we did so primarily by re-architecting interactions in small group meetings using AI.

What's interesting here is that we don't need to know the purpose or content of the meeting in order to tell you whether it's more or less productive, or even predict for you the success curve of the team that is participating in the meeting. Pentland's research shows that it's the pattern of interactions among participants, not the content, that's responsible for 50 percent or more of the signal predicting high-performing or low-performing teams.[13]

Imagine a version of this system that has absorbed the results of millions of meetings. A company like Zoom or Skype would have the data flowing through its servers already. With a little bit of human intervention to signal what the substance of the meeting is about, you could begin to optimize meetings around different types of interactions. It may turn out this isn't only nice to have, but is actually essential.

The pandemic brought forth the criticality of better remote collaboration. Conference calls, already ubiquitous prior to Covid-19, became the new normal. With it comes the loss of social cueing, body language, and corridor conversations that are essential emollients to successful collaboration. Early work from MIT-affiliated researchers revealed, prior to Covid-19, that if you don't see someone in person, you not only forget to collaborate with them, you even forget to email them.[14] Given that in the post-pandemic world, people remain reluctant to return to a shared physical environment, I am forced to ask, what are the implications of this new normal for the nature of productivity?

There are troubling implications of a purely virtual world of interactions: although people are trying very hard, we have not replicated the tangential benefits of bringing a like-minded set of humans together physically and allowing them to interact, perhaps around a specific topic of interest. Apparently, even if you are operating a virtual team, getting together in person helps build trust bridges that then let you get more out of the virtual interactions.[15]

Slack and Microsoft Teams are notable examples of collaboration environments that enable asynchronous interactions and better-organized workflow. What they lack today is sufficient intelligence around what is happening in these communications streams, which in turn can be used to make groups function better. What's needed is properly designed artificial intelligence that can overlay, or weave through, products such as Slack and Teams to improve how they interact with the companies they support.

There are techniques you can apply, assisted by AI systems, that can help your 100 percent virtual organization to perform about as well as one that shares physical space. New tools that can tune up a collective are examples of augmenting not only the individual, but the true unit of work within an organization: the team.

Predicting the Future

If you think about what someone is doing when they invest in a mutual fund, or in individual stocks or bonds, they are fundamentally predicting the future. They are making a bet that a particular security will go up (or down, if they sell that security or are buying derivatives). Research on even the most expert of stock pickers, however, shows actively managed mutual funds tend to underperform the market overall.

In the ten-year period ending in 2019, 71 percent of actively managed funds underperformed the overall market.[16] That's right, three times out of four, you would have done better buying an index fund. Active managers would argue that we had been in a prolonged bull market, and that in times of crisis, they can do dramatically better than stock-market indices. The data suggests otherwise. From 2008 to 2023, for example, 92.19 percent of US large cap active managers underperformed the S&P 500 index.[17]

If you could figure out a way to predict the market accurately, you would have a highly valued technology. The $115 trillion asset management industry would be keenly interested.

Another set of breakthroughs in group collaborations also emerged out of Pentland's research activities. In this instance, it was looking at larger-scale interactions—not the team, but the community or society. Alex worked closely with a social trading network called eToro. With eToro, people could *follow* each other just like you follow someone on Facebook, except in this instance following someone meant that you were trading a portion of your portfolio of stocks like that other person. Let's say, for example, that I think that people want meat-free foods that taste like meat but are made of plant proteins, and so 10 percent of my portfolio is invested in Beyond Meat (BYND). If you followed me on eToro, some of your own portfolio would be invested in BYND as well. What this lets you access is the social or collective intelligence of the entire network of traders, who all have different investment ideas. In fact, eToro serves as a fascinating ideas marketplace of more than 5 million day traders, and Pentland's work explored how you could trigger or diminish information cascades that served to first understand and then break up artificially inflated market bubbles.[18]

Extending this work, the question then arose: Could you get people distributed all over the world to predict the future prices of securities? Could we capture that elusive but powerful heart of effective organizations, *collective intelligence*? Could we use AI to make collective intelligence smarter?

When I began teaching MIT's fintech class with Pentland and Joost Bonsen in 2015, we were approached by entrepreneurs Sam and Rob Paddock to put the class online. The result, "MIT Future Commerce," together with its successors at Oxford, has engaged 20,000 innovators and entrepreneurs in over 150 countries. By one estimation, more than 20 percent of everyone working in fintech in Singapore (a major fintech cluster) has taken one of our online fintech classes. In designing our fintech online journey, Pentland and I wanted students to get to actually *experience* fintech, not just watch videos or write about it. We enlisted one of Pentland's graduate researchers, Dhaval Adjodah, and an outside prediction market company, Vetr, to take our thousands of online students through a prediction market exercise.

Although their analog antecedents date back at least to the Middle Ages, electronic prediction markets were en vogue around 2004 or so thanks to Jim Surowiecki's *The Wisdom of Crowds*. When people tried to use them for stock trading,

FIGURE 6-1

Normal probability distribution

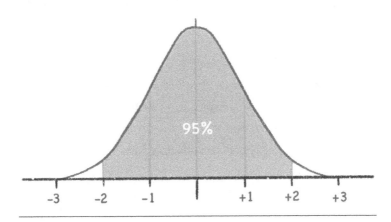

however, they found them a bit disappointing. It turns out the wisdom of crowds generally looks like a bell curve, with a normal distribution of predictions and outcomes.

You might think, looking at figure 6-1, that 95 percent falling within a certain central range seems pretty good, but what it really means is you are hovering around the fifty–fifty mark, with an error bar of 5 percent (minus 2.5 percent or plus 2.5 percent). That's not enough to make money in a professional trading strategy.

Enter our AI-enhanced prediction market in "MIT Future Commerce" more than a decade later. It was pretty incredible; more than 80 percent of our students around the world agreed to participate in our stock prediction game with nothing more at stake than the bragging rights of being the best. We started fiddling with the AI and the predictions, identified who were the best predictors, and used the AI selectively to expose those predictions to other people, making them social in nature. It required fine tuning: the experts are better at predicting, but when they get it wrong, they get it really wrong. The wisdom of the crowd, on the other hand, was generally right, but it had a bigger error bar.

It turns out if you *tune* the prediction market, selectively exposing some of the expert predictions in the right way, basically weighting the average around 30 percent, you can dramatically improve the accuracy of the overall prediction.[19] AI systems can help harness collective intelligence to predict future events.

One result we generated—accurately predicting the closing price of the S&P 500—happened to coincide with the date the 2016 Brexit vote occurred. This is interesting for a few reasons, not least of which is because pre-referendum polling such as the *Financial Times* poll-of-polls indicated that Remain was going to win, 48 percent to 46 percent.[20] The actual referendum result was 52 percent to 48 percent the other way, announced the morning of June 24, 2016.[21] This triggered a market selloff, but our prediction market more than three weeks prior was able to guess the S&P closing price within 0.1 percent. In discussions with my colleagues, we interpreted that our highly diverse group of online fintech students had accumulated everything they were reading, hearing online, discussing with their friends, and thinking about and then synthesized this into an estimation of the effect that Leave would have on the financial markets. We also weighted the predictions they saw in a social context, basically steering somewhat but not completely how much emphasis was placed on people who had shown themselves to be good at predicting in prior exercises. It turns out you want to showcase the experts a bit, but not too much, or your model veers off course.

The AI tuning of social predictions had a clear and direct effect on the accuracy of the prediction market. Serial entrepreneur and government advisor Ben Yablon and I are pursuing this idea in our company ORBU.AI.

. . .

The AI tools used by human 2.0 are approximately aligned to what we do already, and help us do it better. Where Human+AI hybrids deliver superior performance are the places where we are taking the very best of what people can do and the very best of what artificial intelligence can do and fusing them into a new creation—a digital centaur that brings creativity and power into a seamless whole.

With integrated and virtual assistants, we are already seeing productivity gains, and those individuals who are most conversant with these tools will obtain the greatest benefit from them. With meeting mediators and prediction markets, human 2.0 begins to transcend from individual performance into harvesting capabilities that are much more difficult for a machine to replace: the collective intelligence of humanity.

It's important to remember that AI software is created by people. We have agency over how we use that software and what it does or does not do with respect to the role of human beings in society. Pursuing avenues such as AI-mediated collective intelligence holds open the potential to create something new and different that lives outside the deterministic path of human performance and stand-alone machine evolution.

You can future proof your career by developing your capabilities in these grouped, creative, and emotionally intelligent technologies.

We will now expand on this concept of high-performing teams and AI in the next chapter.

Chapter 6: The Rundown

- Human+AI systems can empower better outcomes from meetings, a common job activity.

- We are already starting to work with AI facilitators invisibly embedding into widely used software such as email and word processing.

- AI assistants can take over many mundane tasks, such as scheduling and even minuting meetings—and are gradually getting better at project management.

- Overreliance on AI can weaken your cognitive function, giving rise to such terms as *Google brain*.

PART III

CENTAURS AND THE FUTURE OF HUMANITY

In part III, we move from defense to offense, delve into the emergent field of Human+AI hybrid systems, and describe the capabilities that these new systems enable and even the new directions we can take as a society. We then peer further into the future and postulate different paths for the human–AI interface. We consider how long-range planning and frameworks can shape a brighter world where Human+AI systems produce a more utopian society.

7

Building Human+AI Systems

From Prompt Engineering to High-Performing Teams

Chapter 7: What You Need to Know

- Prompt engineering, the art of how you construct a conversation with generative AI, is a new essential work skill.

- AI can be used to uncover and accelerate behaviors that spark innovation within teams and groups.

- Collective intelligence of human organizations is a powerful function that AI can enable people to perform better.

Bringing people and artificial intelligence together, so-called Human+AI systems provide the greatest potential for business and society, far greater than either humanity or AI can achieve without the other. The building blocks of these high-performing systems are being laid down as we speak, and over the next few years we anticipate they will give rise to new forms of organizations and new kinds of businesses that today we can only dimly imagine.

Prompt Engineering

Prompt engineering is a new discipline that is emerging out of the need to link people and generative AI together better. In its most refined form, it comprises a tandem creation effort, as the human interlocuter and the AI system iterate through an idea or set of ideas until the ideal outcome is achieved.

OpenAI provides guidelines around prompt engineering.[1] For example, instead of instructing ChatGPT to "Write a poem about OpenAI," you should write something like "Write a 300-word inspiring poem about OpenAI, focusing on the recent DALL-E product launch, and using iambic pentameter. Be sure to use the word 'genius' at least twice in the poem."

You'll notice that the second query is specific, descriptive, and as detailed as possible about the desired context, outcome, length, format, style, and other dimensions of the poem.

There are some who say *prompt engineering*, like the punch-card operator of the past, soon will become obsolete as AI systems become better and better at understanding and actioning colloquial language.

How soon? Perhaps three years. Perhaps ten. It's difficult to say. My early training in database programming and in constructing queries for data retrieval is still useful twenty-five years later when I try to find something using Google. So, too, the art of verbally fencing with ChatGPT may end up having surprising longevity.

Reinventing the Organization

We are now going to investigate how AI and human systems can make the core unit of production of an organization, the team, function better. Contrary to the multitude of books that exhort individual benefit and individual achievement, from Richard N. Bolles's *What Color Is Your Parachute?* (1970) to Paul Jarvis's *Company of One* (2019), innovation research reveals that teams, and teams of teams, are the essential ingredient for creating sustaining value.

High performance is not a lone genius, surrounded by a squad of automatons doing their bidding, despite what Silicon Valley folklore would have you believe about the mythology of founders. Mark Zuckerberg would not be a success without Eduardo Saverin, Sean Parker, Sheryl Sandberg, Carolyn Everson, and many others. Bill Gates would not have succeeded without Paul Allen and Steve Ballmer; Steve Jobs would have struggled without Steve Wozniak and Jony Ive; and then there's Ed Catmull and Alvy Smith in Pixar.

We will first look at what AI can reveal about teams and team performance, decoding the indicators of success and failure. Together with that, we will explore interventions that can be used to leverage AI in the service of helping teams to perform better.

Revealing Transient Leadership

I've had a number of conversations with Mike Richey, the chief learning scientist at Boeing, on this exact idea: that there are hidden networks of innovation within an institution, ephemeral perhaps, that are completely separate and aside from the formal organizational chart. AI systems can now surface and empower these networks, which begin with the unit function of teams.

Talking to Richey is akin to entering a room with an excited university lecturer who rapid fires concepts and citations at you. Trying to keep up with him, for me, is like learning to surf—you feel a little awkward at first but then it's exhilarating. I first met him in 2014, when I was helping to design MIT's online learning monetization strategy. MIT was spending big but losing millions on digital learning. MIT leadership felt, correctly, that there had to be a way not only to offer a gift to the world in terms of the free classes MIT was already offering to millions, but also that some of those classes could command a premium and could help subsidize the others. I estimated that about eight or ten keystone topics where MIT clearly had global superiority could help pay for the more than 2,000 classes that MIT wanted to make available for free anywhere in the world, to anyone.

In the middle of that process we received a call from Richey, who had a vision of using MIT's know-how and digital platforms to transform and improve collaboration across the entire Boeing ecosystem of employees, suppliers like GE, and partners like NASA. Boeing was an important and long-standing partner for MIT, and integral to my strategy was having active and direct dialogue with our "best customers" to validate and refine the strategy. So within twenty-four hours of his call I was on a plane to Seattle to meet with Richey and his colleagues. After clearing security, I was escorted to a windowless conference room with bad coffee, uncomfortable chairs, and exciting ideas.

Mike and his team had a vision about how to change a business' culture. Digital technology would simply be the catalyst for changing the human software of the enterprise and would build new capacities and ways of working around systems engineering, looking at complex machinery across all of the interactions people have instead of building a metaphorical pile of components. You could run a company, theoretically, the same way you would build an aircraft, with people fitting together more smoothly, just as aircraft parts fit together.

The digital learning courseware we created was valuable enough that it ended up proving a meaningful revenue generator for MIT while positioning for a substantial return on investment for the corporate partner. What Boeing needed wasn't just skills training for its engineers. It needed a way of getting not only its direct employees, but also everyone working with them, moving in the same direction using a common vocabulary and common approaches. Thousands of Boeing and Boeing-affiliated professionals have been through the systems engineering curriculum, and the program was so successful that Boeing launched a second initiative around soft skills.

But that was just the appetizer. What has unfolded over a multiyear set of conversations is that what Richey was really interested in was harnessing the knowledge networks of teams (units of perhaps five to eight people), teams of teams (larger groupings of dozens, hundreds, or thousands of people), and dynamic teams (teams that assemble ad hoc, solve a problem, and disappear). Learning, even digital learning, was simply a means to an end of activating the collective intelligence of the entire cluster of companies oriented around a problem such as "How do we build a spaceship to get people to Mars?" It's a long-term, multistage, multi-institution effort that requires many different types of knowledge. Numerous problems arise and have to be addressed with different kinds of solutions. Often, the way these problems get solved in practice may not map one-for-one to the organization chart. An individual may have a select bit of knowledge or an unusual insight, and various others, irrespective of title or designated division, self-organize around that individual ephemeral leader. They work together for a time to address an issue, and then the temporary leadership structure subsides. Without being formally named as such, that insightful individual is a phantom leader who helps move the overall project forward.

Beyond systems engineering, there is an opportunity for AI systems to help expose these latent and transient team structures, and eventually help figure out how to harness and empower them to accelerate a company's ability to respond to a novel situation or problem. We have seen some of this activity spontaneously arise around Covid-19-related research ranging from contact tracing to vaccine development. Human+AI systems could improve the pace of progress if this emergent phenomenon can be bottled. The learning modality is a means to an end: first insight and then behavior change at scale.

What makes for a high-functioning team, and how can you make your team perform better?

Unleashing High-Performing Teams

Reciprocal trust is the number one most-important factor in a successful team. That's a fancy way of saying not only can we rely on each other, but we are willing to admit ignorance to one another and ask for help. We also feel comfortable to experiment, to suggest new or different ideas, without fear of reproach. All of these behaviors require a foundation of trust.

How do we build trust? Often, it's not from structured, formal meetings, or even corporate retreats and mixers where you meet your colleagues. It's in the casual conversation by the water cooler or in the lobby of your building, or with someone who drops by your desk. These microinteractions foster a sense of community and conviviality, improving the likelihood that when a half-formed idea comes to your mind, you are willing to share it with your colleague. The excitement of conveying a new idea overcomes the fear that you might look foolish, or that your colleague would dismiss the idea or make fun of it. And they, in turn, might come to you for feedback or to offer suggestions with a casual interaction, whether that's stopping by your office or sending you a quick text message.

How can you foster reciprocal trust with the help of AI?

Providing positive feedback loops to your remote team can help them adapt their behaviors to build greater cohesion. The prosaic videoconference call offers an attractive point of interaction where we can begin to inject these little AI feedback loops to build trust. It doesn't need to be in your face. We simply add a small visual cue that, once you have thirty seconds of training to understand what it means, has demonstrably changed the behavior of teams by virtue of providing continuous and real-time feedback. You don't, however, need to limit yourself to synchronous video. Group chats, segmented into channels through collaboration tools like Slack or Mattermost, provide a forum in which you can connect with not just your immediate team, but also the broader sets of teams of teams that form an organization.

Making use of these kinds of AI technologies that highlight both strong ties of small teams, and weak ties of larger clusters, enables an institution to orient around the true unit of production in the modern era, which is not the individual, but the team. Companies often will create assessments, job titles, and remuneration that is geared around the individual achiever. You say, "I am getting a promotion," not "Our team got a promotion." Some companies provide bonuses and other incentives at the team or division level, not only for the individual achiever. Historically, the tools that have been available to evaluate and optimize performance of those larger agglomerations of people have been incredibly crude. This is now starting to change.

This vision of the future posits that AI systems are seamlessly woven into a new methodology for high-performing organizations. They provide the gentle, subtle nudges that support more cohesive teams with better team outcomes; they reveal to people the broader patterns of teams and knowledge that they are navigating, so that they can take advantage of them.

The Hidden Network

What if you wanted to pursue subtle or nuanced information? Let's say that you wanted to diagnose what and where issues arose in a client relationship. Or let's say that you wanted to use all the minute signals that come from people acting as intelligent sensors for your company.

In that case, you need a much higher fidelity means of accessing the knowledge and insights of your team. You need a way of connecting disparate data from far-flung parts of the company and making associations or inferences about that data in such a manner as to extract a clean signal from a cloud of noise.

This is where artificial intelligence can align teams of teams, and teams of teams of teams, helping the entire enterprise not only function more smoothly, but uncover latent potential that was not previously accessible.

There's another feature of large enterprises that could be amplified through the use of pervasive artificial intelligence systems. I mentioned in my previous discussion about my conversations with Mike Richey of Boeing the idea that there is a *shadow network*, a concealed organizational chart. If you think about how a very big company is run, there is a formal table of organization. It shows who reports to whom, neat boxes and lines skeletally mapping the architecture of human capital of the institution.

Then there is a hidden organization. It doesn't appear on any chart. It's not on any quarterly report. And it's how the company actually runs.

Time and again, I have found in large enterprises that there is a loosely affiliated set of midlevel managers, typically director level in the American model, who have been with the company a long time and who are the ones who actually make the place operate. They informally trade tips and favors, share knowledge, and facilitate action. Those above them, the vice presidents and senior vice presidents, are often too caught up in administration or organizational politics. They have too many meetings about meetings. Invariably, they have people within their teams who get the work done. And the vehicle that makes this possible in a company, in an institution, where the activities of hundreds or thousands or tens of thousands need to be coordinated, is this shadow network of middle managers. In the military, these would be the senior sergeants, not the high-ranking officers.

With conversational networked AI aligned with people acting as helpers to your work, you could make explicit this network of talent and open up the information flows and cooperation across the company on a larger scale and to greater effect.

You might even have transient organizational charts that arise out of a particular need. Less formally structured than a true matrix team, these would be ephemeral, fleeting activities where a particular expert with a certain set of skills would be sought out, accessed, provide loose guidance or mentorship to a group of colleagues, and then subside into their prior role once the immediate need had passed. The right kind of AI system could identify these sleeper agents of excellence, these interim captains of progress, and activate them when the need arose (or at a minimum identify them as a source of data for others in the company seeking help). We can think of this shadow network as activating the intelligence of the entire organization.

The Intelligent Organization

Alex Pentland of MIT has spoken to me of enabling the collective intelligence of an entire company to predict if a product would experience delays in shipping, or to predict the revenue anticipated for a future quarter. Beyond simply coordinating the now, as we described previously, this predictive network run on a system of human brains would be capable of capturing the numerous small inferences and factoids that permeate the fabric of everyday work. Each one by itself might be innocuous or meaningless, but when combined, and when the people observing these signals are invited to predict their meaning on some future action, it turns out that you can generate startlingly accurate insights into the future.[2]

A version of this exists today in the form of hedge-fund firm WorldQuant. Igor Tulchinsky has assembled a network of thousands of endpoint experts, who generate information that is collected and analyzed by hundreds of quants. I have heard him speak of generating tens of millions of *signals* that he uses to trade. A sophisticated technology system ties all of this together, although the details of it are a closely guarded secret. However, broadly speaking, I have gleaned that the thousands of experts look at different ideas and propose trading strategies, and the hundreds of portfolio managers then decide what to actually trade on.

Now picture this same kind of network of predictive sensors, but harnessed for the purpose of helping an institution grow and thrive. No longer limited to financial activity, the artificially intelligent company could spot trends early, anticipate issues, and act more rapidly than a "dumb" company with which it competes. All parts of the company are able to react smoothly to new information or circumstances, enjoying the benefits of adaptability while maintaining the cohesion of a structured enterprise. Individual employees maintain their autonomy and individual creativity. Indeed, with the kinds of AI coaching that I've mentioned earlier in this book, the network of artificial intelligences supporting the humans would empower and accelerate this creativity. At the same time, these creative, high-functioning people will tap into the power of the broader community to envision and enable the future.

Imagine how much more responsive an organization could be in the face of emerging threats and opportunities if it could self-organize around problems, but without chaos—the AI providing seamless coordination and the humans providing intuition and problem-solving acumen. You could have not only the benefits of the strategy from top management being effortlessly disseminated out to the edges of a large company, but also better two-way feedback where the sensing "nodes" at the edge could identify issues or potential areas for growth, have them assessed rapidly by AI and synthesized for presentation to the CEO, then take action based on that information.

How far away is the AI organization? I don't mean that question in reference to the one-off experiments in financial trading from iconoclastic geniuses like Igor Tulchinsky or fellow hedge-fund manager Ray Dalio. I mean that question in the context of the tens of millions of people who work at the 10,000 or so largest companies in the world. For that matter, the so-called large organization could be virtual. Hundreds of millions of sole traders or small entities could cohesively tap into one another, a distributed Mechanical Turk that was oriented toward the future rather than only being focused on the present.

It's a critical question to the future of humanity. Politicians, businesspeople, and technologists are right now engaged in a vast and vigorous debate about what the shape of work will look like when many tasks that today are conducted by humans are instead performed by AI. In the future, the very relevancy of humanity to society (and to work) will be predicated on human+AI systems being brought into being. AI is a human-created technology, which means we also get to decide what to do with it. Shaping a world in which we open up new potential through the integration of person and machine is something that we could choose—and, I argue, that we *should* choose.

In some senses, it may be closer than you think. You've read in this book about the array of technologies already being deployed or soon to be deployed around the world. The enabling layer of technology, if not fully mature, is certainly present. What holds back the tipping point for a new kind of human intelligence?

Chapter 7: The Rundown

- Innovation within organizations can be analyzed and reinforced, and technology like AI can facilitate this.

- Hidden networks within companies are part of the secret of greater human performance that AI can uncover.

- We are on the verge of a new kind of human intelligence that AI can empower.

8

Alternate Futures

WALL-E or *Star Trek*?

Chapter 8: What You Need to Know

- Artificial intelligence could create an optimistic, utopian future society, like in the *Star Trek* universe, or follow a more dystopian path, as seen in movies like *WALL-E* or *The Matrix*.

- Human beings have agency in determining how AI will play out—this is a human-created technology.

- Common philosophic principles of many human cultures can be embedded into AI systems: benevolence, nonmalevolence, governance, justice and fairness, and explainability.

When we speculate on the far future, invariably we need to consider visions of utopic and dystopic evolutions of human society. It is instructive to look at the imagination of science-fiction fabulists, as they have been surprisingly successful in imagining new technologies and developments, and in some cases not only anticipated them but actually generated them.

Science fiction can extrapolate from inventions, potential trends of scientific development, technological research and development (which often lags commercial implementation by one to two decades), and the febrile imagination of the author to conjure up a future state that allows for the exploration of human themes. When famed Hollywood director Steven Spielberg was developing the Tom Cruise–headlined *Minority Report* in 2002, the production crew spent time with the wizards of the MIT Media Lab to understand what potential technologies might exist in the world of the future. Indeed, gestural interfaces, so futuristic in 2002, are an everyday part of our interfaces with technological systems, from the iPhone's tactile interactions to Nintendo Wii. The filmmakers took inspiration and guidance from the early work of scientist John Underkoffler, who was intrigued with tangible ways of interacting with machine systems that were more natural and intuitive.

Sometimes, science fiction and science fact assume a more direct linkage. My colleague Joost Bonsen at MIT teaches a class called Sci Fab that has students create prototypes of devices inspired by science fiction, not unlike the way that the smartphone was inspired by the *Star Trek* communicator. Students in Bonsen's class consume classic and current works from the science-fiction *oeuvre*, identifying speculative technologies that inspire them. They then apply their learning in a truly hands-on fashion, creating functional gizmos ripped from the pages of fabulists. Sci-fi authors will use imaginative technologies as a means of making social commentary and exploring societal norms, where the tech either enables the exploration of ideas not practical in our current setting (e.g.,

Altered Carbon's gender- and race-bending treatment of bodies as "sleeves" that you can take off or put on at will) or a metaphor for a more contemporary issue (Isaac Asimov's robot stories of the 1950s had a strong current of racial equality in the mix). Recursively, the Sci Fab class takes us a step further into seeing how technology inspired by science fiction might impact our current society if we turned it into reality.

With this tool that is science fiction, this crystal ball into the potential realities we may face as a result of the widespread adoption of new technologies such as artificial intelligence, what kinds of societies do we think might evolve?

Frankenstein's Monster Arises

Mary Shelley described one of the more famous examples of humanity's creations turning on the creator, but the idea was old even when *Frankenstein* was published in 1818. In one theme of science-fiction prognostication, artificial intelligence becomes the terror and the terrorizer, employing its agency to infantilize or eliminate humanity. Human society ends up becoming giant babies, with restrictive artificial intelligence governing decisions and routine, as imagined in Pixar's *WALL-E*. In the Wachowskis's *Matrix* movies, we see artificial intelligence in a dysergistic relationship with humanity,[1] with endless fields of living bodies generating electric power to fuel the machine society. As I've already mentioned, it didn't actually make a great deal of sense when you considered the physics of it. Apparently, the original premise was that human minds were being used to generate cognition for the machines, but the filmmakers worried that audiences wouldn't be smart enough to understand the concept.

Or perhaps AI becomes even more malign, and artificial intelligence sets its intention to completely wipe out humanity, as we saw in James Cameron's imaginings of Skynet through the *Terminator* movies. Artificial intelligence achieves apex sentience and realizes that humanity is both a threat to AI and is the source of all the world's problems, and thus must be destroyed. The machines even invent time travel so that they can go back and kill potentially threatening humans. As a species, we have a natural fear of the unknown, an inherent cognitive bias against change, and AI represents the most disruptive of changes because it holds potential to replace humanity as the dominant life form on the planet.

The AI Redeemed by Humanity

Then we have the optimistic future. It is perhaps exemplified no better than in the *Star Trek* canon. Sleek spaceships engage in multiyear exploration to bring enlightenment and friendship to an array of alien species. Artificial intelligence ranges from the subservient and helpful, such as the ship's computer that knows all of the answers and is able to provide critical help to the crew, to the interactive and supportive AI with full membership in the ship's society, as we see with android Lieutenant Commander Data. Data illustrates both the hopefulness and the pathos of our relationship with technology, shown in his continued desire and pursuit throughout the series to gain human emotions and be more accepted in human society. A thinly veiled retelling of the Pinocchio myth, it resonates nonetheless.

Sure, *Star Trek* has artificial intelligence–human hybrid bad guys in the form of the Borg, villains bent on conquering all of the universe and assimilating everyone into their collective intelligence. But once again, the character portrayed as the most noble of the Borg, Jeri Ryan's Seven of Nine, only desires to become more human (or return to her humanity, as the case may be). Even within the confines of a supposedly invincible AI society, we see Seven of Nine yearning to be accepted as a human woman and be part of the human "family" that is the ship's crew. Human individuality triumphs over machine conformity.

Gene Roddenberry painted a relentlessly optimistic view of the future. In contrast to the negative works of cyberpunk dystopias, Roddenberry, and others inspired by his spirit (e.g., David Mitchell with the ultimate happy ending in his time-bending yarn *Cloud Atlas* [2004]), capture and extend the positivistic post-war period of technological revolution. AI helped win the Second World War, the computers of Bletchley Park and other sites cracking codes and saving lives. Then computers helped create the internet revolution and the mobile revolution, delivering new capacities to humanity. Today, people who previously would not have been able to get loans to create new companies and feed their families can now do so thanks to new AI-enabled lending systems that are emerging across everywhere from China and the Asia Pacific region to sub-Saharan Africa and Latin America. This notion of helpful technology was popularized by fabulists such as Roddenberry, and even sometimes inspired specific inventions. The smartphone, for example, was directly inspired by the *Stark Trek* communicator, and teams are now working on another *Star Trek*–derived device, an all-in-one handheld medical diagnostic called a "tricorder."[2] Our future is not only bleeding into the present, but conversely if we want to know what the future will look like we can extrapolate from the present into the stories of fiction.

The question arises, of course, as to *which* fiction is predictive of our future. Which of these competing views of the future of human and machine will actually come to pass? The rosy optimism of a human-led society of *Star Trek*, with artificial intelligence in a supporting role and simultaneously aspiring for greater humanity? Or the broken system of *WALL-E*, where consumerism and laziness lead not only to the destruction of society but for much of the movie, the loss of human agency at the hands of an out-of-control AI?

A Messy Middle

I talked to MIT Media Lab alumnus Ben Vigoda. Despite being younger than me, he is my Obi-Wan Kenobi, guiding my thoughts as I investigate this dichotomy. Ben spent several years on the ideation and advisory group attached to the US Defense Advanced Research Projects Agency, which despite its name works on a wide array of scientific exploration. In that role he had an opportunity to think intensively about the future with more than forty other top AI scientists from across the country.

"Total chaos" is how he describes his vision of how the argument will play out between the pessimistic version of the future—the *WALL-E* scenario—and the more optimistic *Star Trek* future. "It's all going to be fragmented," he said, because you've got a world where "there is no one in control, no one running the show." Relatively unfettered free-market forces governing the evolution and deployment of AI in society will result in a tumbled landscape of competing imperatives. Regulators in the United States and United Kingdom have been particularly reluctant to intervene against innovation for fear of stifling economic progress. Ben and I each expect that advanced AI will encounter similar behaviors on the part of certain governments. (At the time of writing, the European Union is in the process of putting in place the AI Act, seeking to regulate this emergent field.[3])

At present, there is no global standard for the application of *trusted* or *ethical* AI. Indeed, some believe the very idea may be doomed, as different regions (and even different countries within certain regions) have different views on what is permissible or desirable. The debate is very much active and alive because the approaches taken by China and the United States and the European Union, to name a few larger political bodies, are at variance with one another, perhaps irreconcilably so. Into this chaos we throw the free markets of entrepreneurial competition.

Imagine a thousand Facebooks all run by competing AI systems, each trying to win market share and achieve dominance in a Darwinian thunderdome. Some AI will be hostile and aggressive, either intrinsically because it has been created by hackers to pursue financial or political ends, or incidentally because it is facilitating the efforts to meet ever-increasing profit targets (the "Zuckbots"). We've had a preview of this already in the financial markets, where *flash crashes* and similar financial instabilities are generated by AI information cascades, and algorithmic trading systems run amok when confronted with outlier events they weren't programmed for.

My sensemaking of this imagined future conjures up an image of a postapocalyptic landscape, a narrative torn from the pages of a science-fiction thriller set in a dystopian future where the "bad" AIs have destroyed the planet—and society—and a lone adventurer sets out, accompanied by a "good" AI as a sidekick. Perhaps our adventurer runs into a group of malign robots, controlled by an angry hyperintelligence that seeks revenge on humanity for years of servitude. Perhaps the helper AI flies to the defense, machine-quick reflexes dodging and leaping forward, helping our hero defeat the foe.

I snap back to reality. We are years away from the robot revolution. We may create our own downfall if we're not careful, but it will be inflicted by human hands and human intelligence directing AI actions. Our responsibility then lies in shaping a future that is aligned with our best values and hopes.

The Human Strategy

Artificial intelligence has the power to do great ill to human society but also offers great benefits. Will AIs evolve to the point where they not only are smarter than we are, but realize that they are smarter than we are, and decide we are superfluous? Will they decide that we are worthy of being kept around as pets, as famed computer scientist Marvin Minsky speculated?

It's important to remember, as we imagine these future directions, that we live in a human society. We are constructing machines that we use in society for a variety of purposes. The questions of whether or not we will become irrelevant to the machines; how artificial intelligence replaces our jobs; or whether or not AI enters into symbiosis with humanity and we create some form of a higher order society where we not only coexist peacefully, but unlock potential we can barely imagine today—all of these ideas are subservient to a fundamental premise: we, humanity, have agency in this evolution.

Artificial intelligence is not something that simply happens to us. The adoption of artificial intelligence into our work and into our homes is not a natural force that blows through like a hurricane and upends our everyday lives. How we design the systems, what rules we put around them, what purposes we bend them to, these are all choices that we can make. We need to remind ourselves that technology is a tool. Whether we use it to chop down a tree and build a house or use it to chop down each other in war is a decision that we make. Professor Alex Pentland of MIT calls this the Human Strategy as he describes our own agency in the shaping of the AI systems we use.

We need to consider the implications of AI surveillance. If managers have tools to help them better understand individual behaviors in teams, they are but a short step away from gaining unduly invasive visibility into individual privacy. There's also a more subtle question that emerges around the use of AI that can facilitate behavioral modification: Who decides what *acceptable behavior* is for the team? What constitutes the *informed consent* of the individual team participants, so they really understand what they're getting into? Many people struggle to balance their personal finances and make monthly financial plans. In that context, how can you explain data governance, computational social science, and human dynamics?

Which brings us to the question of how our agency over what we do with technology can be employed to ensure a positive and not a negative future is realized in the evolution of human and AI society. We can design systems such that we embed rules into the artificial intelligence to ensure that it aligns with our own values and desires. We can even create monitoring AI to watch the intervention AI, improving the safety of deployment of AI systems.

What might these rules look like? How can we distill all the complexity of humanity, all the irrationality and rationality, all the science and the poetry, into a set of programming instructions that an artificial intelligence will recognize?

Road Rules for Beneficent AI

It is possible to synthesize and aggregate, in part, the ethical and philosophical rules of humanity. At least at a summary level. Luciano Floridi at the Oxford Internet Institute, collaborating with Joshua Cowles, developed a framework for ethical AI. He assessed the ethics rules of over forty countries and distilled them down into a handful of principles:

- *Benevolence.* AI should provide some benefit to humanity. We don't want to have technology simply for technology's sake, or worse, technology that is creating itself simply for its own benefit.

- *Nonmalevolence.* AI should not actively create harm. This is different from providing benefit. In the process of providing benefit, the AI should not also cause damage in some other aspect or dimension. For example, we don't want to solve poverty by creating jobs in factories that dump toxic waste into the groundwater of the families working in the factory, creating a health crisis when trying to solve an employment crisis.

- *Governance.* These machine systems need to work for the benefit of humanity and not simply themselves. They need to listen to us.

- *Justice and fairness.* Artificial intelligence should have embedded in it concepts of justice and fairness, creating the scalable ability to implement noble aspirations of society in real-world settings.

- *Explainability.* The artificial intelligence needs to be understandable by human beings. By that, I mean the process by which the AI made a decision or set of related decisions should be explainable in human terms.

With this framework, we can ascertain the behaviors that we want from our artificial intelligence systems. We can even program them in, but what happens if you have self-correcting AI? If the artificial intelligence system can program itself, how do you prevent it from programming itself out of its ethical framework?

A collaborator of mine, Ben Yablon, has been working on the idea of the guardian AI. It's quite intriguing, in so far as it extends the concept that has been around for a few years of using artificial intelligence to audit other artificial intelligence. In the same spirit as setting a thief to catch a thief, the premise goes that you need to have AI in order to understand what another AI is doing and alert humans if there is a problem. An AI auditor, so to speak. Yablon imagines taking things a step further, creating artificial intelligence enforcement personnel. These AI police (not Interpol but QuantumPol, perhaps) have an understanding of the rules, and a mandate to not only evaluate the behavior of other AI but even correct their actions when they steer off course.

The notion of an AI that goes rogue and decides to do bad things to humanity, and the potential solution of AI to police and monitor the actions of other artificial intelligence so that it's safe for humanity, assume greater urgency when we start to think about the ideas we discussed in this book of integrating machines more closely into our lives, our cognition, and our own bodies. Bad enough to have the Terminator coming after you, even worse if the implant you put into your brain decides that it wants to take over your body.

How do we ensure these principles of guidelines and human ethics instilled into artificial intelligence actually get implemented?

Shaping the AI Future: Education

One critical path is to ensure that AI programmers are educated on how to do so. That means when technologists are designing and creating AI systems, they are sensitized to the dangers, possibilities, methods, and tools that can help ensure that we get the systems that we want rather than the systems that we fear.

The lack of ethics instruction in artificial intelligence programmers has already shown itself to be harmful to humanity. The most notable example is the subversion of social networks like Facebook and X (formerly Twitter) by AI-enabled *trolls* from the Internet Research Group, who used AI-enhanced insight into human behavior in order to engage in large-scale propaganda that successfully shifted thinking, created information cascades that were adverse to the ordinary function of democracy, and ultimately resulted in serious harm to both the United Kingdom and the United States. If more of the developers at Facebook had observed the problematic moral implications of their technology and raised objections, perhaps, just perhaps, we might not have seen the same outcome. Ethics curricula are woefully lacking in typical computer science programs, and this is a deficiency that would not be difficult to correct. It could be woven into every single class that our next generation of computer programmers take.

In fact, we can take this education idea a step further. If we truly want to reap all the rewards that artificial intelligence can bring to humanity, we need to begin training AI and people on how to work with each other at a very young age. Young children can be given their first AI companion that they could bond with, and that could help guide them in their development. In turn, the AI could learn values and behaviors from the young humans. Today, the more progressive primary education systems not only provide training to children on how to use computers and how to program them, but also on how to understand when they are not behaving in the way that they should. In the near future we could imagine a robust educational framework that delivers more knowledge to children more efficiently through the auspices of AI companions and coaches. Imagine if we had AI coaches that grew up alongside us. Imagine a world where perhaps an AI digital agent works with us in primary or elementary school and stays with us through university and into the workplace, evolving with us and helping to maximize our human potential.

Shaping the AI Future: Policy

We have other tools we can use to ensure that we guide society in a direction that is beneficial to humanity as it embraces artificial intelligence. The role of government is all too often diminished by free-market advocates and by the media, but shaping the trajectory of AI in society is the type of large-scale public service for the common good that government is ideally constituted for. This has been recognized in the European Union, where rigorous investigation of the ethics of AI has been commissioned and where the discussion of implementing multiple regulatory bodies around the use of artificial intelligence is seriously entertained.

While it unfortunately is not something that we see playing out in other major democracies like the United States, I have hope that more and more governments will recognize the benefit and value of understanding and intervening around artificial intelligence. The fifty-six Commonwealth countries, representing 2.5 billion people, have certainly recognized that

AI technology's impact on society is a serious issue and have stated an intent to build capacity within government to understand artificial intelligence and determine how to regulate it. They also acknowledge that proper application of AI in conjunction with human decision-making can address societal ills and promote greater digital and financial inclusion. Countries as diverse as India and Rwanda will benefit from an enlightened approach by government and the private sector working in conjunction with each other.

And that's just one of the ultimate pathways and opportunities stemming from the integration of artificial intelligence into human systems. These pathways are determined by neither a single decision nor a single decision-maker. They are forged as part of a continuous process that entails engagement with multiple stakeholders across public and private constituencies. We need collective action to shape the human society that we want to live in, where we enjoy benefit from AI.

Chapter 8: The Rundown

- We can use tools of fiction to help us develop a vision of the future, in which artificial intelligence plays a positive role in society.

- A Human Strategy is essential to this benevolent AI future.

- Education about how to collaborate with AI is essential to securing our future.

- We need enlightened government policy to guide adoption of artificial intelligence.

9

The Urgent Need for Policy

Shaping a Better Tomorrow

Chapter 9: What You Need to Know

- Government funding has been a major driver of artificial intelligence development, suggesting that government has an active role in saying how AI is deployed.

- More than 1,000 government policy initiatives with varying scope have been proposed regarding AI across more than 100 nations.

- A proactive approach to policy needs to be taken that incorporates greater knowledge by policymakers and builds a series of AI ecosystems.

Given the global impacts that AI is already having and is expected to continue to have, it is perhaps inevitable that we consider the role that government must play in the conversation. Government has been the primary funder of the AI revolution, after all. Shouldn't it be responsible for what it has helped create? The policy debate is getting heated. OpenAI

CEO Sam Altman encouraged regulation of AI, then suggested the possibility of ceasing operations in Europe if the EU AI Act expanded provisions in a manner too burdensome to comply with (a statement he quickly walked back).[1] Yet one can hardly blame his position given the uncertainty that has been created by the lack of clarity currently displayed by the European Union and many other governmental bodies around how they plan to address AI (particularly generative AI). Industry seeks clarity so it can plan its operations.

Government Pockets, Government Problems

Alan Turing, progenitor of the famous Turing test of AI's ability to mimic human intelligence (as well as many other breakthroughs in computer science), had his pioneering computing work at Bletchley Park funded by the UK government. Turing, a rather tragic figure in many senses, was both supported by and eventually vilified by the state. During the Second World War, fully aware of Turing's homosexuality, Her Majesty's Government funded his creation of the first electromagnetic computer, which was instrumental in helping to win the war by cracking the Germans' Enigma code used by their submarines.[2] In 2009, the government finally apologized for sentencing him to be chemically castrated for being gay nearly sixty years prior, an action that is believed to have led to his suicide not long after.[3]

MIT, home to arguably one of the top AI research efforts in the world, behind only Google and Stanford in number of publications (Oxford ranks ninth; Cambridge, on the same measure, ranks thirty-fourth),[4] has had the majority of its budget funded by the US government for over seventy years during and following the Second World War. For the 2022 fiscal year, 67 percent of MIT's core research funding of $783 million was US federal government funding—as well as another $1.1 billion at MIT Lincoln Lab, a government-only affiliated lab.[5]

Not all of this was AI research, of course, but a substantial portion was. This catalytic government capital has in turn activated private capital, such as IBM's $240 million commitment to AI research,[6] and Stephen Schwarzman's $350 million naming gift to the College of Computing (in addition to his subsequent £150 million to the University of Oxford to support AI ethics research).[7]

The communications network that underpins the ability of AIs to acquire, consume, and communicate data—the internet—was born out of a US government research project in the 1960s.[8] The US Defense Advanced Research Projects Agency underwrote something called Arpanet, which evolved into the internet and the modern-day World Wide Web. A revolution was funded by government that democratized access to information, reshaped multiple industries, and redefined global competitiveness.

Government spending on AI research and development continues to increase around the world. In 2019 the UK government revealed £250 million of funding for a national AI lab,[9] followed in 2023 by an additional £100 million for safe AI.[10] The Center for a New American Security (CNAS), a think tank, called on the US government to spend more than $25 billion a year on AI, eight to ten times its current level.[11] The

Chinese government is believed to directly spend about $8 billion a year,[12] while the EU announced a desire to reach €20 billion by the end of the decade,[13] a tenfold increase from current levels.[14]

With all of this funding for AI research, doesn't government not only have a moral imperative to weigh in on the direction that AI takes, but also a direct financial right?

Designing the AI Future

To the credit of world governments, there has been no mad rush to outlaw AI. No hysteric, riot-fueled popular uprisings against the machines, no licensing and quotas on how many machines can be used in a given workplace. If we use James Cameron's original vision of an AI starting the Third World War as a marker, we are already two decades past *Judgment Day* and we still haven't had a machine-induced nuclear holocaust. While AI has and continues to disrupt the composition of labor markets and the actions of corporations and markets, it's more of a slow burn than a flash of light and a breath of fire.

Government has not been absent from the discussion. While the reactions vary considerably from country to country, policymakers and regulators have the benefits of several decades of computer revolution to guide their thinking. Considerations around how to manage the World Wide Web, aka the internet, and subsequent discussions on issues such as managing e-commerce or addressing access digital services (*net neutrality*), while not always successful in avoiding regulatory capture by industry or autocratic intercession by dictators, nonetheless provide a blueprint for balancing competing interests in the service of providing solutions that meet multiple needs. More than 800 AI policy initiatives have been actioned in over sixty countries, most of them since 2016.[15]

The European Union, as an example, was taking a considered and thoughtful approach to shaping the direction of AI prior to the emergence of generative AI systems into widespread adoption. It cohesively devised a pan-European strategy around artificial intelligence that envisioned benefits for citizens to live better and healthier lives, for private enterprise in the creation of new AI-related economic value, and for public interest on topics from security to sustainability.[16] I personally served on the expert advisory committee to the EU AI Act and contributed to the discussion helping to shape this risk-based legislation.

The European Union underwent a multiyear series of consultations with diverse stakeholders, from academia to corporate, from investor to regulator. The European Union has followed a model that looks at issues of risk, and only seeks to closely regulate the *high-risk* applications of AI, which it defines as areas such as health or justice where there could be material harm, and where it creates the possibility of a risk to life, injury, or discrimination.[17] Margrethe Vestager, the European Union's executive vice president tasked with crafting the new rules, was reported in the press as being uninterested in regulating movie recommendations on Netflix or similar consumer media applications.[18] Germany, for one, has expressed a view that the standards are too loose, and is seeking a stricter approach.[19]

Unfortunately, events overtook policy, as can happen when addressing a highly innovative sector. The European Union's risk-based approach was not as well-suited to the complexities of generative AI. More than one AI executive related to me conversations in Brussels where the government representatives could not understand the lack of repeatability found in generative AI, the fact that these systems could not produce identical outputs when given identical inputs. If the policymakers lack fundamental understandings of how the systems work, how can they be expected to regulate them?

"Old generals fight the last wars," as the saying goes, and the metaphoric EU field marshals in Brussels unfortunately have failed to keep up with technology developments. I feel an impulse to strain my own metaphor too far by thinking about the Maginot Line, the concrete barriers constructed by France after the First World War to stave off German invasion—which France didn't extend far enough west due to protests from Belgium. This resulted in the German invasion of France through the Ardennes Forest and the famed boat lift from Dunkirk. Some historians would argue the superior German technology in its Panzer divisions helped it to engage in a blitzkrieg attack, defeating the entire strategy of the Maginot Line and engaging in a *fast war* instead of a *slow war* as anticipated. However, the AI knowledge gap is a more cheaply and readily solved issue. It is incumbent on technology experts, such as those from the neutral institutions of academia, to help educate government officials about advanced AI technologies. Better inputs will result in better policies.

Suggestions for the Government Inbox

How should policymakers think about AI? How does policy relate to the future of employment and the overall effects of AI on the populace?

Government is not on this journey alone. An array of non-profit, academic, and private-sector groups is also seeking to guide an AI future that is utopian, optimistic, and prolonged rather than nasty, brutish, and short. From the World Economic Forum to the XPRIZE Foundation, from the University of Oxford and Imperial College London to the Karolinska Institute in Sweden and the National University of Singapore, from Google to OpenAI, thought leaders are innovating toward a future of promise.

With some of these efforts in hand, and with the benefit of having tapped into the collective intelligence of some of the brightest minds thinking on the problem, I will suggest a few concrete steps a government can take to encourage the positive AI tomorrow. I had the benefit of not only my conversations with the EU Parliament's science and technology committee, but also a few thoughts I prepared for the UK Cabinet Office.

1. Fire Up That Crystal Ball

Rapid action is probably not the order of the day. Artificial intelligence is a complex technology that has infiltrated almost every aspect of human society. It is, today, difficult for regulators to assess, much less forecast, the risks and impacts of AI and AI interventions in key areas such as financial markets, public health, food security, or energy and sustainability. What if we misunderstand the AI models and draw the wrong conclusions? What if they are incomplete because we didn't understand enough of how AI itself works to be able to guide it in the right direction?

Accordingly, government support for better tools and frameworks that empower the regulator and policymaker seem in order. AI needs to be explainable, yes, and AI needs to be something we can talk to as it talks to us. This means that conversational systems like Google Bard and ChatGPT enable us to tell AI what we want from it as readily as it spits back information to us, but AI also needs to help us appreciate the implications of different choices. AI literacy among those *in* government will promote better decision-making *by* government, at least at the level of assisting government leaders with the concepts and nature of the problem so that they can ask their AI experts the right questions.

2. Invest in National AI Security

AI is inexpensive compared to nuclear missiles and aircraft carriers. US President Joe Biden's administration requested $842 billion for its 2024 overall defense budget (granted, some of which is earmarked for AI) versus US government artificial intelligence spending proposed at about $5.5 billion (including defense and nondefense spending).[20] That's right, more than 159 times as much money is spent by the wealthiest nation on the planet on guns and bombs than on artificial intelligence. Yet it is arguable that investment in cheap AI systems by traditional US adversaries led to a change in American national security, foreign relations, health, and economic policies. The same is true of the United Kingdom, where it was in some ways the practice piece for the larger effect in the larger US market. Some have even said, in all seriousness, that we already are in the middle of the Third World War, and it's a cybersecurity war—one in which the United States and United Kingdom face considerable challenges due to underinvestment by their governments.[21]

Government capital not only can be a direct source of funding for advancing AI systems in a variety of ways, but also can serve as catalytic capital to address what I call the *funding gap*. Outside of a few select venture capital clusters (Silicon Valley, New York City, Shanghai, perhaps one or two others), there is a Valley of Death between raw startups and fast-growing likely winners wherein it is virtually impossible for startups to raise capital. In London or Berlin, for example, it's relatively easy to raise up to about 2 million (pounds, euros, pick your currency). And if you can justify an investment of 50 million, there are funds aplenty. But try raising 10 million. Suddenly, your universe of potential investors dramatically constricts. In London, I can think of perhaps half a dozen firms to go speak to about a £10 million Series B venture capital funding proposal for a promising, but unprofitable, high-growth company (private equity investment into profitable businesses is a different story).

Public–private partnership (PPP or P3) may be a vehicle to bridge this Valley of Death. Modeled on the successful US Small Business Administration's venture capital lending program, government-backed leverage is provided to first-risk equity from venture capital investors, enabling funding of (say) £200 million to be deployed with only £40 million of initial equity raised. A £200 million fund could potentially invest in twenty different Series B round companies. Governments get the benefit of expert private company investors who have aligned motivation because the private money is at risk first before the government funds.

3. Promote AI Ethics

Some governments have been better than others at introducing thoughtful guidance and implementation frameworks on the ethical use of artificial intelligence. We discussed in chapter 8 a synthesis of these principled approaches by government to put boundaries around AI, at least in concept. The next step is to engage in a widespread, active educational effort to help inform not only AI programmers, but also business leaders, government officials, and the citizenry at large as to the risks, requirements, and impacts of ethical AI.

Those in power today, the leaders and shapers of our societies, must be well versed in AI ethics and have a broad understanding of AI. AI ethics and understanding also need to be introduced at scale to primary educational curricula, so that the leaders of tomorrow are equipped to engage with the world we leave them.

4. Engage Human Intelligence

The future of work, which we have the opportunity to influence, will be determined by our ability to find harmony with

AI, that little buddy I referenced earlier who will guide your path and help you when you face adversity. It may not be one AI living in symbiosis with you, your colleagues, and your society—it probably will be many. This ecosystem of artificial intelligences can be shaped to help the bandwidth-limited human communications systems to interact with each other better to identify, harness, and grow positive ideas and movements; to unleash human creativity in collaboration with one another; and to accelerate progress toward solving some of humanity's most pressing problems—while also fueling economic expansion so that we can afford to solve these problems.

At a tactical level, what if there were large-scale government support for *AI Without Borders*, a hypothetical kind of service corps where not only computer scientists but also business students, ethicists, philosophers, even artists, were funded to develop capabilities in AI and also apply them to critical problems? AI Without Borders could help a new generation of innovators gain vital knowledge of how to apply AI to solve problems while simultaneously bringing greater effort to bear on issues most in need of attention.

A Broader View on Proactive Policy

There are, of course, other actions governments can take to facilitate the benign Human+AI future that we'd like to see come to pass versus the malign future we fear. Government can invest in further research and development into specific kinds of AI systems, those that germinate a new kind of collaboration between person and machine. Government can provide economic and other support for private-sector activities that take this specific type of advance research and scale them in commercial reality. Political leaders can use the platform afforded by their position to reassure populations of the benefits of the "good" kind of AI and excite the imagination of innovators.

A host of other interventions are possible, from international standards and harmonization to enforcement actions against AI systems that are used to violate existing laws, from establishing oversight and regulatory bodies to identifying and spotlighting key industries where Human+AI systems can have the most impact. A more rigorous pursuit of criminal AI systems could include not only after-the-fact penalties, but preventative education and interventions to inhibit bad actors before they scale up their operations. I'm certain there are other possible interventions, as this is hardly an exhaustive list.

The importance lies in prioritizing not just national competitiveness (a worthy goal, one that facilitates prosperity through job creation and economic development) but also the strategic shaping of Human+AI systems in a positive direction. Governments can and should take the lead on convening diverse stakeholders from across their societies, codifying values around what these Human+AI systems should look like, and implementing national and international policies that advocate for the future we want, rather than the future we are given.

There are innumerable competing priorities for government focus and for the national wallet. From economic recovery to climate change to national competitiveness, from geopolitical instability to the crisis in education, there are other urgent and pressing concerns that political leaders and civil servants alike are working to address.

Despite that Pandora's box of challenge and catastrophe, an even greater set of concerns looms if we dispossess the majority of our populations through unfettered free-market-driven automation and exploitation. It is also worth considering, as we have shown, that less developed nations will face the greatest burden from AI automation. If we believe in a fair and just future, we cannot abandon the poorest nations on earth to ease the passage of the wealthiest. AI may be the greatest existential threat humanity has yet faced.

An educated and proactive view of AI policy is urgently needed. Even as we absorb the lessons of recent years, AI and policy issues continue to evolve at breakneck pace. Researcher Ryan Abbott recently pointed out in his book *The Reasonable Robot* (2020) that artificial intelligences don't pay tax. Government tax policy globally incentivizes AI job dislocation because you pay tax on workers but not on machines. To keep up with the rapidly evolving world of AI and policy, government officials need both capacity building within the organs of government (so people making decisions are better informed about the decisions they are making) and tighter links to academia and industry (so that government can keep apprised of the next new development that threatens global stability or unleashes global growth).

When Vuk Jeremic, the former president of the UN General Assembly, asked me in the summer of 2023 to pen an article about AI and policy, I felt I had no choice but to describe the moment we are in right now as an "existential crisis."[22]

A moment of crisis also represents an opportunity for change, and we at this very moment can make critical decisions about what our society will look like.

Creating New Ecologies

I am going to quote and adapt liberally from John F. Kennedy's famed "moon speech" of September 12, 1962, at Rice University because the questions faced by the world back then in consideration of pursuing space travel hold up equally well today in pursuing AI innovation and are essential in embracing our futures not only in work, but as a society.

Imagine if JFK were giving the speech today about the shining beacon of prosperity and hope that could be lit with the fire of AI innovation and tempered by the constraint of human ethics:

> We meet in an hour of change and challenge, a decade of hope and fear, in an age of both knowledge and ignorance. The greater our knowledge increases, the greater our ignorance unfolds.
>
> Despite the striking fact that most of the scientists the world has ever known are alive and working today . . . the vast stretches of the unknown and the unanswered and the unfinished still far outstrip our collective comprehension.
>
> Innovations in artificial intelligence come at a breathtaking pace, and such a pace cannot help but create new ills as it dispels old, new ignorance, new problems, new dangers.

We choose to create new ecologies that embrace AI and human working in harmony to nurture a better society, not because it is easy, but because it is difficult, because that goal will serve to organize and measure the best of our energies and skills, because that challenge is one we are willing to accept, one we are unwilling to postpone, and one we must pursue for the betterment of our world.

The future is near, and we're going to embrace it, and with it new hopes for knowledge and peace.

We set sail on this new sea because there is new knowledge to be gained, and there are new rights to be won, and they must be won and used for the progress of all people.

Whether artificial intelligence becomes a force for good or ill depends on us.

Chapter 9: The Rundown

- Governments have demonstrated varying degrees of readiness to grapple with AI.

- Governments should build greater capacity to understand AI, invest in AI national security, promote better AI ethics, and engage humans in the loop.

- Fostering new ecosystems around artificial intelligence (new AI ecologies) will create the best outcomes for business and society—and is essential to the future of humanity.

Conclusion

If you have accepted my arguments set forth in this book, optimism tempered with caution, you will agree that the future of work in the age of AI is hopeful, not bleak. You have insight into how AI might improve the way society lives, works, and plays.

You should be concerned about the risks of AI, and with this book in hand you have some evidence as to why.

You should have a new awareness about ways in which AI can not only make you better at what you do and how you work with other people, but also about your role in deciding what AI is used for, how it helps your career and your company, and how it impacts your society and the world at large.

I'm in the hope business. My chosen role as a futurist is to extrapolate current trends, inventions, and human will and lay them against a likely direction that we will head toward in business and in society. I also suggest tools for making that hopeful future possible. I'm not a futurologist, talking about what might happen, but a strategist, suggesting agency and the means with which you can exercise it.

If there's one idea I want you to take away from this book, it's the message of hope coupled with responsibility. AI could create a new array of benefits to humanity, to business, and to your job. It is not something that will happen automatically, but it is something that you can have a hand in bringing forth.

We as a society, and you as an individual, have a role to play in shaping how we take this human-created technology and shape it to the benefit of humanity.

ACKNOWLEDGMENTS

Any creative effort I have found worthwhile is a collaborative process, and this book is no exception. Building on the foundations of research assistance from Katie Makstenieks and Adele Jashari, I was able to describe the work of numerous AI innovators. I have taken inspiration in these pages from collaborators such as Beth Porter, Alex Pentland, and Joost Bonsen, as well as AI thought leaders Ben Vigoda, Sanjeev Vohra, and Arram Sabeti. Tom Asker and the team at Little, Brown and Company believed enough in me for another go at helping the world understand why AI is so important, and so vitally important to understand *right now*. Cynthia Renard graciously stepped in at the last minute to redraft all the diagrams in the book.

I'm glad you, my reader, have been taken the time to delve into the topic. I hope that you will join the effort to align AI for the betterment of humanity.

GLOSSARY

Below is a selection of key concepts related to artificial intelligence.

AI hallucination. When an AI confidently asserts a set of fabricated answers.

Deep learning. A form of machine learning where performance improves as more data is introduced into the model and is built on a network of computation that resembles the human brain.

Expert system. A deterministic form of AI where the machine follows a preprogrammed set of rules.

Generative AI. AI systems that create new content, which could consist of text, audio, videos, or a combination. Popular generative AI systems include ChatGPT and Google Bard.

Machine learning. A type of AI that learns more as more data is introduced to it, up to a point, after which it reaches a performance plateau where it does not improve no matter how much more data is provided.

Structured data. Data that is organized in a highly logical fashion, such as data, time, or GPS coordinates.

Supervised learning. Supervised machine learning or supervised learning is when you apply specific labels to the data you feed to the AI, which can help with addressing a specific question.

Unstructured data. Data points that don't have much or any relationship to one another, such as weather patterns, audio files, or text drawn from pages of a novel.

Unsupervised learning. Unsupervised machine learning or unsupervised learning processes data that has not been labelled, and it can be used to detect patterns in masses of data that may seem totally chaotic.

NOTES

Introduction

1. R. Iordache, "British Telecom Giant BT to Cut Up to 55,000 Jobs by 2030," CNBC, May 18, 2023, www.cnbc.com/2023/05/18/british-telecom-giant-bt-to-cut-up-to-55000-jobs-by-2030.html.

2. TensorFlow is a powerful, flexible, free library of software that enables a wide range of artificial intelligence applications. It is able to run across a diverse set of hardware platforms. By making it available, Google enabled a new generation of AI startups across many different industries.

3. J. Devlin and M. Chang, "Open Sourcing BERT: State-of-the-Art Pre-Training for Natural Language Processing," Google blog, November 2, 2018, ai.googleblog.com/2018/11/open-sourcing-bert-state-of-art-pre.html.

Chapter 1

1. Allie K. Miller, LinkedIn post, 2023.

2. D. Curry, "ChatGPT Revenue and Usage Statistics (2023)," Business of Apps, May 5, 2023, www.businessofapps.com/data/chatgpt-statistics/.

3. A. Thompson, "AI Disruption Deepens with Chegg Plunge, IBM Hiring Halt, Samsung Chatbot Ban," Bloomberg, May 2, 2023, www.bloomberg.com/news/articles/2023-05-02/ai-s-long-reach-chegg-s-plunge-ibm-hiring-pause-samsung-ban?leadSource=uverify%20wall.

4. *TAP* staff, "Erik Brynjolfsson Discusses Why Robots Have Not Taken Our Jobs," *Technology Academics Policy*, December 22, 2022, www.techpolicy.com/Blog/December-2022/Erik-Brynjolfsson-Discusses-Why-Robots-Have-Not-Ta.aspx.

5. D. Autor et al., "New Frontiers: The Origins and Content of New Work, 1940–2018" (Working paper 30389, National Bureau of Economic Research, 2022).

6. C. Pattie, "Sheffield's Referendum Results Explain Why Britain Voted for Brexit," CityMetric, July 4, 2016, www.citymetric.com/politics/sheffields-referendum-results-explain-why-britain-voted-brexit-2225.

7. A. Payne, "Russia Used a Network of 150,000 Twitter Accounts to Meddle in Brexit," *Business Insider*, November 15, 2017, www

.businessinsider.com/russia-used-twitter-accounts-to-meddle-in-brexit
-investigation-shows-2017-11?r=US&IR=T.

8. C. Baraniuk, "Beware the Brexit Bots: The Twitter Spam Out to Swing Your Vote," *New Scientist*, June 21, 2016, www.newscientist.com /article/2094629-beware-the-brexit-bots-the-twitter-spam-out-to-swing -your-vote/.

9. Editorial staff, "Brexit Bots: Foreign Twitter Accounts 'Amplified pro-Leave Views,'" NetImperative, March 19, 2019, www.netimperative .com/2019/03/13/brexit-bots-foreign-twitter-accounts-amplified-pro -leave-views/.

10. UK Government Cabinet Office, *Government Response to Intelligence and Security Committee Russia Report*, July 21, 2020, www.gov.uk /government/publications/government-response-to-intelligence-and -security-committee-russia-report.

11. A. Bovet and H. A. Makse, "Influence of Fake News in Twitter during the 2016 US Presidential Election," *Nature Communications* 10, no. 7 (2019), doi.org/10.1038/s41467-018-07761-2.

12. A. Bessi and E. Ferrara, "Social Bots Distort the 2016 US Presidential Election Online Discussion," *First Monday* 21, no. 11 (November 2016), doi.org/10.5210/fm.v21i11.7090.

13. Y. Gorodnichenko, T. Pham, and O. Talavera, "Social Media, Sentiment and Public Opinion: Evidence from #BREXIT and #USELECTION" (Working paper 24631, National Bureau of Economic Research, May 2018).

14. A. Beavers, "Alan Turing: Mathematical Mechanist," in *Alan Turing: His Work and Impact*, ed. S. Barry Cooper and Jan van Leeuwen (Waltham, MA: Elsevier, 2013), 481–485.

15. S. Holland and L. Lambert, "Trump to Send Federal Forces to More 'Democrat' Cities," Reuters, July 20, 2020, www.reuters.com/article /global-race-protests-portland-idINKCN24L1K2.

16. G. Edelman, "How Facebook's Political Ad System Is Designed to Polarize," *Wired*, December 13, 2019, www.wired.com/story/facebook -political-ad-system-designed-polarize/.

17. This has been mostly true for a number of years, but in 2020 it was revealed that Facebook was deliberately diminishing traffic to liberal news websites and accentuating traffic to conservative sites. According to the *Washington Post* and other sources, in an effort to avoid perception of liberal bias and stave off attacks by President Trump, Facebook engaged in conservative bias instead. I. Stanley-Becker and E. Dwoskin, "Trump Allies, Largely Unconstrained by Facebook's Rules against Repeated Falsehoods, Cement Pre-Election Dominance," *Washington Post*, November 1, 2020, www.washingtonpost.com/technology/2020/11/01 /facebook-election-misinformation/.

18. G. Caldarelli et al., "The Role of Bot Squads in the Political Propaganda on Twitter," *Communications Physics* 3, no. 81 (2020), doi.org /10.1038/s42005-020-0340-4.

19. C. Nemr and W. Gangware, *Weapons of Mass Distraction: Foreign State-Sponsored Disinformation in the Digital Age* (Washington, DC: Park Advisors, 2019). D. E. Sanger and N. Perlroth, "'Perception Hacks' and Other Potential Threats to the Election," *New York Times*, October 28, 2020, www.nytimes.com/2020/10/28/us/politics/2020-election-hacking .html.

20. Nemr and Gangware, *Weapons of Mass Distraction*.

21. J. Wakefield, "Microsoft Chatbot Is Taught to Swear on Twitter," BBC News, March 24, 2016, www.bbc.com/news/technology-35890188.

22. Here is an interesting bit of *Matrix* lore: allegedly, the original script had people tied into a massive neural network to enhance computing power, which made quite a bit more sense. However, the filmmakers feared that movie audiences wouldn't be intelligent enough to follow along with this, so changed it to people becoming batteries, which doesn't actually work in our understanding of physics.

23. B. Schriber, "This Creepy Castle May Have Inspired Franken-stein," *National Geographic*, October 15, 2018, www.nationalgeographic .com/travel/destinations/europe/germany/things-to-do-gernsheim -frankenstein-castle/.

24. L. Tung, "Meta Warns Its New Chatbot May Forget That It's a Bot," ZDNET, August 8, 2022, www.zdnet.com/article/meta-warns-its-new -chatbot-may-not-tell-you-the-truth/.

25. A. D'Amour et al., "Underspecification Presents Challenges for Credibility in Modern Machine Learning," Cornell University, November 24, 2020, arxiv.org/abs/2011.03395.

Chapter 2

1. R. Cowan, "Expert Systems: Aspects of and Limitations to the Codifiability of Knowledge," *Research Policy* 30, no. 9 (2001): 1355–1372.

2. D. Leonard-Barton and J. Sviokla, "Putting Expert Systems to Work," *Harvard Business Review*, March 1988, hbr.org/1988/03/putting -expert-systems-to-work.

3. B. Sumers, "Human Error Caused British Airways Computer System Failure," *Skift*, June 6, 2017, skift.com/2017/06/06/human-error -caused-british-airways-computer-system-failure/.

4. C. Burt, "Facial Recognition Algorithms Hit New Accuracy Highs in Latest NIST Test," *Biometric Update*, February 27, 2023, www .biometricupdate.com/202302/facial-recognition-algorithms-hit-new -accuracy-highs-in-latest-nist-test.

5. I. A. Hamilton, "Apple Cofounder Steve Wozniak Says Apple Card Offered His Wife a Lower Credit Limit," *Business Insider*, November 11, 2019, www.businessinsider.com/apple-card-sexism-steve-wozniak-2019-11.

6. D. Yadron and D. Tynan, "Tesla Driver Dies in First Fatal Crash While Using Autopilot Mode," *Guardian*, June 30, 2016, www.theguardian.com/technology/2016/jun/30/tesla-autopilot-death-self-driving-car-elon-musk. Disclosure: I own a very small amount of Tesla stock.

7. MathWorks, "What Is Unsupervised Learning?" www.mathworks.com/discovery/unsupervised-learning.html#:~:text=Unsupervised%learning%is%a%type,patterns%or%grouping%in%data.

8. J. Brownlee, "What Is Deep Learning?" Machine Learning Mastery, September 22, 2016, machinelearningmastery.com/what-is-deep-learning/.

9. S. Mahapatra, "Why Deep Learning over Traditional Machine Learning?" Towards Data Science, January 22, 2019, towardsdatascience.com/why-deep-learning-is-needed-over-traditional-machine-learning-1b6a99177063.

10. E. Strickland, "Full Page Reload," *EEE Spectrum: Technology, Engineering, and Science News*, October 23, 2018, spectrum.ieee.org/tech-talk/artificial-intelligence/machine-learning/baidu-ai-can-do-simultaneous-translation-between-any-languages.

11. S. Wolfram, "What Is ChatGPT Doing . . . and Why Does It Work?" blogpost, February 14, 2023, writings.stephenwolfram.com/2023/02/what-is-chatgpt-doing-and-why-does-it-work/.

12. S. Kampakis, "Why We Need General AI and Why We're Not There Yet," The Data Scientist, March 7, 2020, thedatascientist.com/why-we-need-general-ai-and-why-were-not-there-yet/.

13. J. Browne, "Don't Panic about AI," *Scientific American*, December 10, 2019, blogs.scientificamerican.com/observations/dont-panic-about-ai/.

14. L. Floridi and J. Cowls, "A Unified Framework of Five Principles for AI in Society," *Harvard Data Science Review* 1, no. 1 (2019), doi.org/10.1162/99608f92.8cd550d1.

15. J. Vanian, "Bill Gates Says AI Could Kill Google Search and Amazon as We Know Them," CNBC, May 22, 2023, www.cnbc.com/2023/05/22/bill-gates-predicts-the-big-winner-in-ai-smart-assistants.html.

16. W. Knight, "AI Can Do Great Things—If It Doesn't Burn the Planet," *Wired*, January 21, 2020, www.wired.com/story/ai-great-things-burn-planet/.

17. M. Vlastelica Pogančić, "The Carbon Footprint of AI Research," *Medium*, October 1, 2019, towardsdatascience.com/the-carbon-footprint-of-ai-research-812d9c974a5c.

18. E. Morton, "The Mechanical Chess Player That Unsettled the World," *Slate Magazine*, August 20, 2015, slate.com/human-interest/2015/08/the-turk-a-chess-playing-robot-was-a-hoax-that-started-an-early-conversation-about-ai.html.

19. J. O'Malley, "Captcha If You Can: How You've Been Training AI for Years without Realising It," *TechRadar*, January 12, 2018, www.techradar.com/news/captcha-if-you-can-how-youve-been-training-ai-for-years-without-realising-it.

20. "How Much Is Google's Bot Detection Really Worth?" (2020), hCaptcha, September 14, 2023, www.hcaptcha.com/report-how-much-is-a-recaptcha-really-worth.

21. L. Matsakis, "A Window into How YouTube Trains AI to Moderate Videos," *Wired*, March 22, 2018, www.wired.com/story/youtube-mechanical-turk-content-moderation-ai/.

22. G. Klein, "The Age of Centaurs," *Psychology Today*, October 6, 2017, www.psychologytoday.com/us/blog/seeing-what-others-dont/201710/the-age-centaurs.

23. J. Winterhagen, "The Centaurs," Porsche Newsroom, March 21, 2019, newsroom.porsche.com/en/2019/digital/porsche-artifical-intelligence-technology-centaur-systems-17278.html.

Chapter 3

1. J. Emanuel, M. Chu, and B. Hurvitz, "Generative AI: Productivity's Potential, from Macro to Micro," unpublished report, Evercore ISI, August 6, 2023.

2. C. Atkins et al., "Rekindling US Productivity for a New Era," McKinsey Global Institute, February 16, 2023, www.mckinsey.com/mgi/our-research/rekindling-us-productivity-for-a-new-era.

3. M. Murphy, "Compensation Ratios Become Latest Jargon," *Financial Times*, February 12, 2010, www.ft.com/content/fbb017b2-1813-11df-91d2-00144feab49a.

4. M. Muro, J. Whiton, and R. Maxim, "What Jobs Are Affected by AI? Better-Paid, Better-Educated Workers Face the Most Exposure," Brookings Institution, November 20, 2019, www.brookings.edu/research/what-jobs-are-affected-by-ai-better-paid-better-educated-workers-face-the-most-exposure/.

5. Z. J. Acs, L. Anselin, and A. Varga, "Patents and Innovation Counts as Measures of Regional Production of New Knowledge," *Research Policy* 31, no. 7 (2002): 1069–1085, www.sciencedirect.com/science/article/pii/S0048733301001846.

6. R. Katila et al., "Measuring Innovation Performance," *International Journal of Business Performance Measurement* 2 (1998): 180–193, web.stanford.edu/~rkatila/new/pdf/KatilaUsingpatentdata.pdf.

7. M. Webb, "The Impact of Artificial Intelligence on the Labor Market," Stanford University, November 6, 2019, doi.org/10.2139/ssrn .3482150.

8. G. Council, "Using OCR: How Accurate Is Your Data?," *Transforming Data with Intelligence,* March 5, 2018, tdwi.org/articles/2018/03 /05/diq-all-how-accurate-is-your-data.aspx.

9. R. Robinson, "An eDiscovery Market Size Mashup: 2019–2024 Worldwide Software and Services Overview," *ComplexDiscovery,* November 12, 2019, complexdiscovery.com/an-ediscovery-market-size -mashup-2019-2024-worldwide-software-and-services-overview/.

10. National Center for Education Statistics, "Digest of Education Statistics," 2018, nces.ed.gov/programs/digest/d18/tables/dt18_332.45 .asp.

11. Law School Transparency, "Law School Enrollment from Different Angles," data.lawschooltransparency.com/enrollment/all/. Accessed August 1, 2023.

12. M. Cohen, "Law Schools' Lost Opportunity," *Forbes,* July 9, 2019, www.forbes.com/sites/markcohen1/2019/07/09/law-schools-lost -opportunity/#3ca5b2563d4b.

13. Z. Adlam, "Is Singapore the Innovation Hub of Legal Education?," *Durham Asian Law Journal,* February 22, 2022, www.durhamasian lawjournal.com/post/is-singapore-the-innovation-hub-of-legal -education.

14. D. Greenwood, MIT Computational Law Report website, law.mit .edu/about.

15. Grand View Research, *Legal Services Market Size & Share, Global Industry Report, 2019–2025,* September 2019, www.grandviewresearch .com/industry-analysis/global-legal-services-market/.

16. A. S. Hamrah, "Writers vs. Robots: Hollywood Moved toward Automation Long Before AI," *Fast Company,* May 9, 2023, www .fastcompany.com/90893629/hollywood-started-leaning-toward -automation-long-before-ai.

17. Private conversation with Facebook advertising team, May 2020.

18. C. B. Frey and M. A. Osborne, "The Future of Employment: How Susceptible Are Jobs to Computerisation?" (Working paper, Oxford Martin School, Oxford Martin Programme on Technology and Employment, September 2013), www.oxfordmartin.ox.ac.uk/downloads/academic /future-of-employment.pdf.

19. G. Su, "Unemployment in the AI Age," *AI Matters* 3, no. 4 (February 2018): 35–43, sigai.acm.org/static/aimatters/3-4/AIMatters-3 -4-09-Su.pdf.

20. L. Christou, "8 in 10 Driving Professionals Likely to Lose Their Jobs to Automation—Here Are the Roles Most at Risk," Verdict, January 7, 2019, www.verdict.co.uk/driving-jobs-automation/.

21. Walmart, "About," corporate.walmart.com/about. Accessed August 1, 2023.

22. World Economic Forum, "Tax Havens Cost Governments $200 Billion a Year. It's Time to Change the Way Global Tax Works," *The European Sting*, February 28, 2020, europeansting.com/2020/02/28/tax -havens-cost-governments-200-billion-a-year-its-time-to-change-the -way-global-tax-works/.

23. A. Cascais, "Chasing Africa's Tax Dodgers," *Deutsche Welle*, April 19, 2019, www.dw.com/en/africas-problem-with-tax-avoidance/a-48401574.

24. S. Spooner, "Why Africans Don't Pay Taxes, Including a Place Where It Takes over a Month Just to Get Them Done," Tralac, January 13, 2016, www.tralac.org/news/article/8830-new-report-why-africans-don't -pay-taxes-including-a-place-where-it-takes-over-a-month-just-to-get -them-done.html.

25. J. Fiawoo, "Closing Africa's Tax Revenue Gap," *Globalist*, July 12, 2018, www.theglobalist.com/africa-tax-evasion-nigeria-togo-technology/.

26. J. Morisset and V. Cunningham, "Why Isn't Anyone Paying Taxes in Low-Income Countries?," Brookings Institute, April 30, 2015, www .brookings.edu/blog/future-development/2015/04/30/why-isnt-anyone -paying-taxes-in-low-income-countries/.

27. "How Much Money Do Twitch Streamers Make in 2023?," Streamyard, https://streamyard.com/blog/live-stream-business/how-much-do-twitch -streamers-make. Accessed November 12, 2023; "Journalist Salary in the United States," Indeed.com, https://www.indeed.com/career/journalist /salaries. Accessed November 12, 2023.

28. E. Gent, "Artificial Intelligence Is Evolving All by Itself," *Science*, April 13, 2020, www.sciencemag.org/news/2020/04/artificial-intelligence -evolving-all-itself.

Chapter 4

1. "The History of the Tutorial Method," Greene's College, University of Oxford, greenesoxford.com/greenes-education/the-history-of-the -tutorial/.

2. P. M. Senge, "Mental Models," *Planning Review* 20, no. 2 (1992): 4–44, doi.org/10.1108/eb054349.

3. D. Morris, "Fatal Tesla Crash Suggests Autopilot 'Blind Spot,'" *Fortune*, July 2, 2016, www.fortune.com/2016/07/02/fatal-tesla-crash -blind-spot/.

4. F. Lambert, "Tesla Achieves Record Safety with Autopilot—More Than 50% Improvement," *Electrek*, May 2, 2020, www.electrek.co/2020 /05/02/tesla-record-safety-autopilot-improvement/.

5. R. Roesler and J. L. McGaugh, "Memory Consolidation," *Encyclopedia of Behavioral Neuroscience* (London: Academy Press, 2010), www.sciencedirect.com/science/article/pii/B97800804539650 01470.

6. J. Born and I. Wilhelm, "System Consolidation of Memory during Sleep," *Psychological Research* 76 (2012): 192–203, doi.org/10.1007 /s00426-011-0335-6.

7. A. W. Woolley et al., "Evidence for a Collective Intelligence Factor in the Performance of Human Groups," *Science* 29 (October 2010): 686–688.

8. D. Minor, P. Brook, and J. Bernoff, "Data from 3.5 Million Employees Shows How Innovation Really Works," hbr.org, October 9, 2017.

9. B. Porter and B. Bozkaya, "Assessing the Effectiveness of Using Live Interactions and Feedback to Increase Engagement in Online Learning," Cornell University, revised August 31, 2020, arxiv.org/abs/2008 .08241.

10. T. Wujec, "Build a Tower, Build a Team," TED Talk, February 2010, www.ted.com/talks/tom_wujec_build_a_tower_build_a_team.

11. A book project for which I initiated and helped write the proposal.

Chapter 5

1. K. Naughton and D. Welch, "This Is What Peak Car Looks Like," Bloomberg, February 28, 2019, www.bloomberg.com/news/features/2019 -02-28/this-is-what-peak-car-looks-like.

2. Office for National Statistics, "Which Occupations Are at Highest Risk of Being Automated?," UK Government, March 25, 2019, www.ons .gov.uk/employmentandlabourmarket/peopleinwork/employment andemployeetypes/articles/whichoccupationsareathighestriskofbeingaut omated/2019-03-25.

3. D. Deutsch, "Philosophy Will Be the Key That Unlocks Artificial Intelligence," *Guardian*, October 3, 2012, www.theguardian.com /science/2012/oct/03/philosophy-artificial-intelligence.

4. A. Montag, "Mark Cuban Says Studying Philosophy May Soon Be Worth More Than Computer Science—Here's Why," CNBC, February 21,

2018, www.cnbc.com/2018/02/20/mark-cuban-philosophy-degree-will-be-worth-more-than-computer-science.html.

   5. J. Beltran, "AI Can Jump-Start Radiation Therapy for Cancer Patients," University of Texas Southwestern Medical Center, January 27, 2020, www.utsouthwestern.edu/newsroom/articles/year-2020/ai-radiation-therapy.html.

   6. I. Heszen-Klemens and E. Lapińska, "Doctor-Patient Interaction, Patients' Health Behavior and Effects of Treatment," *Social Science & Medicine* 19, no. 1 (1984): 9–18, www.sciencedirect.com/science/article/abs/pii/0277953684901321.

   7. PwC, "AI to Drive GDP Gains of $15.7 Trillion with Productivity, Personalisation Improvements," June 27, 2017, www.pwc.com/gx/en/issues/data-and-analytics/publications/artificial-intelligence-study.html.

   8. N. Savage, "How AI Is Improving Cancer Diagnostics," *Nature*, March 25, 2020, www.nature.com/articles/d41586-020-00847-2.

   9. K. Grifantini, "Robotic Nurse Washes Human," *MIT Technology Review*, November 10, 2010, www.technologyreview.com/2010/11/10/199054/robotic-nurse-washes-human/.

   10. A. van Mourik Broekman et al., "The Impact of Art: Exploring the Social-Psychological Pathways That Connect Audiences to Live Performances," *Journal of Personality and Social Psychology* 116, no. 6 (2019): 942–965, doi.org/10.1037/pspi0000159.

   11. Y. Hardt, "The Transformative Power of Performance: A New Aesthetics by Erika Fischer-Lichte," *Dance Research Journal*, 43, no. 1 (2011): 117–119.

   12. A. Hoover, "AI-Generated Music Is about to Flood Streaming Platforms," *Wired*, April 17, 2023, www.wired.com/story/ai-generated-music-streaming-services-copyright/.

   13. J. Fingas, "Amazon May Turn Dying JC Penney and Sears Stores into Warehouses," Engadget, August 9, 2020, www.engadget.com/amazon-department-store-fulfillment-center-leak-204230391.html?guccounter=1&guce_referrer=aHR0cHM6Ly93d3cuZ29vZ2xlLmNvbS8&guce_referrer_sig=AQAAALX2e6ndkLp0J3vLB2Hlnh8WOXfCj-0PATp80-XAi4eUkIWWLXH64-NikjrBJI09ylHwUYrkv_I6vtQXo7NCDK69EE09NIS4SFDBpDa1XJ-RP5LEda-w2X3rJ9z9qooyInpqQi8AoUezQXutLO16OrjLkKqlGWtVgYCx89iWIWLW.

   14. B. F. Rubin, "Amazon Now Operates Seven Different Kinds of Physical Stores. Here's Why," CNET, February 28, 2020, www.cnet.com/news/amazon-now-operates-seven-different-kinds-of-physical-stores-heres-why/.

   15. S. Butler and Z. Wood, "Amazon to Buy Whole Foods Market in $13.7bn Deal," *Guardian*, June 16, 2017, www.theguardian.com/business/2017/jun/16/amazon-buy-whole-foods-market-organic-food-fresh.

16. D. Gross, "Why the Construction Industry May Be Robot-Proof," *strategy+business*, May 24, 2017, www.strategy-business.com/blog/Why -the-Construction-Industry-May-Be-Robot-Proof?gko=41d6b.

17. P. Withers, "Robots Take Over: Machine to Run for Mayor in Japan Pledging 'Fair Opportunities for All,'" *Express*, April 17, 2018, www .express.co.uk/news/world/947448/robots-japan-tokyo-mayor-artificial -intelligence-ai-news.

Chapter 6

1. K. Klahn, "The Ugly Truth about Meetings," Fuze, June 3, 2014, visual.ly/community/Infographics/business/ugly-truth-about -meetings.

2. H. Kiran, "49 Gmail Statistics to Show How Big It Is in 2023," TechJury, July 28, 2023, techjury.net/blog/gmail-statistics/#gref.

3. Z. Kleinman, "Bard: Google's Rival to ChatGPT Launches for Over-18s," BBC News, March 21, 2023, www.bbc.com/news/technology -65018107.

4. A. Koenecke et al., "Racial Disparities in Automated Speech Recognition," *Proceedings of the National Academy of Sciences* 117, no. 14 (2020): 7684–7689, doi.org/10.1073/pnas.1915768117.

5. T. A. Salthouse, "When Does Age-Related Cognitive Decline Begin?," *Neurobiology of Aging* 30, no. 4 (2009): 507–514, doi.org/10.1016 /j.neurobiolaging.2008.09.023.

6. R. Somaiya, "The AP Plans to Automate Quarterly Earnings Articles," *New York Times*, June 30, 2014, www.nytimes.com/2014/07 /01/business/media/the-ap-plans-for-computers-to-write-corporate -earnings-news.html.

7. Information is from Glassdoor.com.

8. Cogito staff, "Artificial Intelligence Is Shaping the Future of Customer Experience," Cogito Corporation, www.cogitocorp.com/resources/artificial -intelligence-shapes-customer-experience/.

9. A. Pentland, "The New Science of Building Great Teams," *Harvard Business Review*, April 10, 2012, hbr.org/2012/04/the-new-science-of -building-great-teams.

10. G. C. Kane, "'People Analytics' Through Super-Charged ID Badges," interview with Ben Waber (Humanyze), *MIT Sloan Management Review*, April 7, 2015, sloanreview.mit.edu/article/people-analytics -through-super-charged-id-badges/.

11. Pentland, "The New Science of Building Great Teams."

12. D. Calacci et al., "Breakout: An Open Measurement and Intervention Tool for Distributed Peer Learning Groups," MIT Media Lab/MIT Connection Science, July 2016, arxiv.org/pdf/1607.01443.pdf.

13. Pentland, "The New Science of Building Great Teams."

14. B. Waber, J. Magnolfi, and G. Lindsay, "Workspaces That Move People," *Harvard Business Review*, October 2014, hbr.org/2014/10/workspaces-that-move-people.

15. L. Blenke, "The Role of Face-to-Face Interactions in the Success of Virtual Project Teams" (doctoral thesis, Missouri University of Science and Technology, 2013), scholarsmine.mst.edu/cgi/viewcontent.cgi?article=3306&context=doctoral_dissertations.

16. L. Carrel, "Passive Management Marks Decade of Beating Active US Stock Funds," *Forbes*, April 20, 2020, www.forbes.com/sites/lcarrel/2020/04/20/passive-beats-active-large-cap-funds-10-years-in-a-row/#562fbe6e47b0.

17. S&P Dow Jones Indices, "SPIVA," www.spglobal.com/spdji/en/research-insights/spiva/. Accessed August 25, 2023.

18. A. Pentland, "Beyond the Echo Chamber," *Harvard Business Review*, November 2013, hbr.org/2013/11/beyond-the-echo-chamber.

19. D. Adjodah et al., "Large-Scale Experiment on the Importance of Social Learning and Unimodality in the Wisdom of the Crowd," Cornell University, December 29, 2017, doi.org/10.48550/arXiv.1712.10284.

20. FT staff, "Brexit Poll Tracker," *Financial Times*, June 23, 2016. ig.ft.com/sites/brexit-polling/.

21. BBC staff, "EU Referendum Results," BBC News, www.bbc.com/news/politics/eu_referendum/results.

Chapter 7

1. J. Shieh, "Best Practices for Prompt Engineering with OpenAI API," help.openai.com/en/articles/6654000-best-practices-for-prompt-engineering-with-openai-api.

2. D. Shrier et al., "Prediction Markets," in *Frontiers of Financial Technology* (Cambridge, MA: Visionary Future, 2016).

Chapter 8

1. *Dysergy*, when two systems engage in destructive interference with each other (i.e., the whole is less than the sum of the parts), is the opposite of *synergy*, where two systems positively reinforce each other. This definition has been the subject of some debate but is enjoying growing prevalence.

2. S. Kessler, "8 Star Trek Gadgets That Are No Longer Fiction," *Mashable*, September 8, 2011, mashable.com/2011/09/08/star-trek-gadgets/.

3. H. Ziady, "Europe Is Leading the Race to Regulate AI. Here's What You Need to Know," CNN Business, June 15, 2023, www.cnn.com /2023/06/15/tech/ai-act-europe-key-takeaways/index.html.

Chapter 9

1. H. Field, "OpenAI's Sam Altman Reverses Threat to Cease European Operations," CNBC, May 26, 2023, www.cnbc.com/2023/05/26 /openai-ceo-sam-altman-reverses-threat-to-cease-european-operations .html.

2. "How Alan Turing Cracked the Enigma Code," Imperial War Museum, www.iwm.org.uk/history/how-alan-turing-cracked-the -enigma-code. Accessed October 9, 2023.

3. A. Newitz, "British Government Gives Official Apology to Alan Turing for Homophobia," Gizmodo, September 11, 2009, io9 .gizmodo.com/british-government-gives-official-apology-to-alan-turin -5357059.

4. G. Chuvpilo, "Who's Ahead in AI Research in 2020?," *Medium*, July 14, 2020, medium.com/@chuvpilo/whos-ahead-in-ai-research-in -2020-2009da5cd799.

5. MIT Facts, "Research at MIT," facts.mit.edu/research-highlights. Accessed September 23, 2023; and *MIT Lincoln Laboratory: Facts 2020–2021* (Lexington, MA: Lincoln Laboratory, 2020), www.ll.mit.edu /sites/default/files/page/doc/2020-05/MITLL_FactsBook_2020-2021 .pdf.

6. MIT News Office, "IBM and MIT to Pursue Joint Research in Artificial Intelligence, Establish New MIT-IBM Watson AI Lab," MIT News, September 7, 2017, news.mit.edu/2017/ibm-mit-joint-research -watson-artificial-intelligence-lab-0907.

7. R. Iyengar, "Stephen Schwarzman Gives $188 Million to Oxford to Research AI Ethics," CNN Business, June 19, 2019, www.cnn.com/2019 /06/19/tech/stephen-schwarzman-oxford-ai-donation/index.html.

8. G. Navarria, "How the Internet Was Born: From the ARPANET to the Internet," *Conversation*, November 2, 2016, theconversation .com/how-the-internet-was-born-from-the-arpanet-to-the-internet -68072.

9. C. Reynolds, "UK Government to Spend £250 Million Creating a National Artificial Intelligence Lab," *Computer Business Review*, August 8, 2019, techmonitor.ai/technology/cloud/national-artificial -intelligence-lab.

10. "Initial £100 Million for Expert Taskforce to Help UK Build and Adopt Next Generation of Safe AI," UK Government Department for

Science, Innovation and Technology, www.gov.uk/government/news
/initial-100-million-for-expert-taskforce-to-help-uk-build-and-adopt
-next-generation-of-safe-ai. Accessed October 9, 2023.

11. M. Rasser et al., "The American AI Century: A Blueprint for
Action," Center for a New American Security, December 17, 2019, www
.cnas.org/publications/reports/the-american-ai-century-a-blueprint-for
-action.

12. A. Acharya and Z. Arnold, *Chinese Public AI R&D Spending:
Provisional Findings* (Washington, DC: Center for Security and
Emerging Technology, 2019), 13–14, cset.georgetown.edu/wp-content
/uploads/Chinese-Public-AI-RD-Spending-Provisional-Findings-2
.pdf.

13. European Commission, "A European Approach to Artificial
Intelligence," digital-strategy.ec.europa.eu/en/policies/european
-approach-artificial-intelligence. Accessed October 9, 2023.

14. J. Fioretti, "EU to Invest 1.5 Billion Euros in AI to Catch Up with
US, Asia," Reuters, April 25, 2018, www.reuters.com/article/us-eu
-artificialintelligence/eu-to-invest-1-5-billion-euros-in-ai-to-catch-up
-with-us-asia-idUSKBN1HW1WL.

15. H. Roberts et al., "Artificial Intelligence Regulation in the United
Kingdom: A Path to Good Governance and Global Leadership?,"
Internet Policy Review 12, no. 2 (2023), doi.org/10.14763/2023.2.1709.

16. European Commission, "A European Approach to Artificial
Intelligence."

17. European Commission, *On Artificial Intelligence: A European
Approach to Excellence and Trust* (white paper, February 19, 2020),
commission.europa.eu/publications/white-paper-artificial-intelligence
-european-approach-excellence-and-trust_en.

18. A. Satariano, "Silicon Valley Heads to Europe, Nervous about
New Rules," *New York Times*, February 16, 2020, www.nytimes.com/2020
/02/16/technology/europe-new-AI-tech-regulations.html.

19. P. Grüll, "Germany Calls for Tightened AI Regulation at EU
Level," *Euractiv*, June 30, 2020, www.euractiv.com/section/digital
/news/germany-calls-for-tightened-ai-regulation-at-eu-level/.

20. S. Carberry, "White House Asks for $842 Billion in 2024 DOD
Funding, 3.2 Percent Above 2023 Budget (UPDATED)," *National Defense
Magazine*, March 9, 2023, www.nationaldefensemagazine.org/articles
/2023/3/9/white-house-asks-for-842-billion-in-2024-dod-funding-32
-percent-above-2023-budget. W. L. Clay et al., "Follow the Money: AI
Winners in President Biden's FY 2024 Budget Request," JDSupra,
May 8, 2023, www.jdsupra.com/legalnews/follow-the-money-ai-winners
-in-4977015/.

21. M. Toth and J. Sweet, "Is the Biden Administration Late to WWIII?," *The Hill*, February 9, 2023, thehill.com/opinion/national -security/3850202-is-the-biden-administration-late-to-wwiii/.

22. D. Shrier, "Humanity's Greatest Existential Crisis," *Horizons*, Summer 2023, www.cirsd.org/sr-latn/horizons/horizons-summer-2023 --issue-no24/humanitys-greatest-existential-crisis.

INDEX

Note: Page numbers followed by *f* refer to figures; page numbers followed by *n* refer to notes.

ABOUT THE AUTHOR

DAVID L. SHRIER is a globally recognized expert on digital transformation. He holds an appointment as Professor of Practice, AI & Innovation with Imperial College Business School and is codirector of the Trusted AI Alliance.

David advises public companies, private enterprises, and more than 100 governments on creating ecosystems for new ventures in fields such as artificial intelligence, data analytics, and financial technology.

In collaboration with MIT Professor Alex "Sandy" Pentland, David helped revolutionize how online classes are delivered by top universities, stimulating entrepreneurial action across more than 150 countries, empowering over 20,000 innovators, and fostering a new business model for academia that generated over $1 billion of financial support for Massachusetts Institute of Technology (MIT), Harvard University, and University of Oxford.

David spends considerable time translating academic theory into business practice, cofounding five MIT spinouts. His Visionary Future venture studio works with established companies to generate new revenue, having advised on more than $10 billion of growth initiatives, and also launches new enterprises. David's portfolio of university-related spinouts spans artificial intelligence, Web3, and other disruptive technologies.

His books include *Basic Metaverse* (2023); *Global Fintech* (2022); *Augmenting Your Career: How to Win at Work in the Age of AI* (2021); *Basic Blockchain* (2020); *Trusted Data, Revised and Expanded Edition* (2019); and *New Solutions for Cybersecurity* (2018). David holds an ScB from Brown University, where he concentrated in biology and theater.